THE FATHER

To my dad,
whose fatherhood made believing in God
as a good and loving father
the easiest thing in the world.

FR. MARK-MARY AMES, CFR

THE FATHER

30 MEDITATIONS TO DRAW YOU INTO
THE HEART OF GOD

ASCENSION

West Chester, Pennsylvania

Ascension
PO Box 1990
West Chester, PA 19380
1-800-376-0520
ascensionpress.com

Cover design: Ashley Dias

Printed in the United States of America
23 24 25 26 27 5 4 3 2 1

ISBN 978-1-954882-35-5 (paperback)
ISBN 978-1-954882-36-2 (e-book)

CONTENTS

Introduction: The Father's Heart. 1

Part 1: The Father's Delight in Us

1   That's My Son 9

2   The Best Part 13

3   Called by Name. 17

4   Cry Out, "Abba! Father! " 21

5   Wonderfully Made 27

6   All She Had 31

7   Telling Everyone 36

8   Beautiful in His Eyes 40

9   Be with Him 45

10   Without Counting the Cost 49

Part 2: The Father's Care for Us

11 He Loved to the End 57

12 That None Would Be Lost 61

13 Ordination Day 65

14 Abundance 70

15 A Shield 74

16 "All That Is Mine Is Yours" 78

17 The Freedom
    of the Father's Child 82

18 Fighting for You 87

19 His Strong Arms 92

20 He Never Tires 96

Part 3: The Father's Call to Us

21 Taking the Time 103

22 Lost in the Desert 107

23 Dying to Self 112

24 Authority 117

25 Perfect Timing 121

26 A Father's Discipline 126

27 Shattered 131

28 A Heart for the Poor 135

29 End Well 140

30 He Laid Down His Life 144

Conclusion: "Abba, Father" 149

Acknowledgments 151

INTRODUCTION
The Father's Heart

It is one of the most beautiful and powerful images in the history of Christianity: the young St. Francis of Assisi standing in the crowded city square, stripped of everything that his earthly father had given him, entrusting himself and his future to his local bishop. And in the presence of the crowd, his father and his bishop, he cries out, "Now I can truly pray, *my Father* who art in heaven."[1]

The radical totality of this moment, as well as the entire life of St. Francis, has pierced the hearts and minds of Christians over the centuries. But for me, spending time pondering his life, ministering in the formation of young vocations, and working on this book has prompted me to step back from the intoxicating beauty of this moment to ask a sobering question, "What was going on in the heart of the man, Francesco Bernardone, at this moment?"

Francesco ended up in this situation because his earthly father was taking him to the bishop to do to his son what the prodigal son did to his father in the parable—to disown him and take away his rights as a son. After persecution and punishment, Francesco's father was resorting to kicking him out of the family. If anyone had a father wound, surely

---

1. Thomas of Celano, *The Remembrance of the Desire of a Soul*, book 1, chapter 7.

Francesco Bernardone did, and yet he still was able to become St. Francis of Assisi.

My own working hypothesis on the man and the saint is that his radical pursuit of Jesus was ordered toward his absolute, total, visceral determination to personally experience God's fatherhood. And the good news is, his heart would find what it longed for—union with the heart of God, the best of fathers.

My hope is that this book may be a source of grace and encouragement on your journey to knowing the Father's heart so that, with St. Francis, you can pray not only "Our Father" but "*my* Father" as well.

We Have a Father in Heaven

The beauty of the Catholic Faith, revealed in the Word of God and the teachings of the Church, is that it does not simply give us a set of guidelines for self-fulfillment. Rather, Jesus comes to give us the fullness of the truth that we have a heavenly Father who loves us and is the best of fathers. The Church's teachings and her guidance give us the path to enter into and remain in this relationship with God, our Father, receiving the fullness of his grace as we journey through this life toward our eternal home.

Many have had negative experiences with their fathers on earth. Others have not had any relationship with their fathers at all. Perhaps, as a coping mechanism, we have gone through life hiding this pain to the point that we do not know how deeply we desire to be able to call God "Abba," Dad. Or perhaps we have had good relationships with our own fathers, yet we hesitate to come to God and call him Father.

This book is written to help us come to the Father. In this book are thirty meditations that invite the reader to prayer. We hide from God, our Father, because we do not trust in his goodness. To heal this lack of trust, this book seeks to show the heart of God so that the reader may encounter his goodness and realize what it means that we are not orphans but beloved sons or daughters of the Father.

The Example of Earthly Fathers

How can we come to recognize the goodness and love of our heavenly Father? In my own reflection, prayer, and preaching, I have found it extremely valuable to reflect on the actions and attitudes of earthly fathers. Perhaps my reflection is the fruit of my own relationship with my dad. I have been blessed to have a father who provided love and care, along with patience, attentiveness, and delight in me. My dad sincerely was an icon of my heavenly Father, helping me understand my own identity and the love of God the Father for me.

Earthly fathers are called to be icons of our heavenly Father. While we must acknowledge that many fall short of this call, it is the true vocation of a father to reflect and point to the heart of God. When earthly fathers accept their vocation to fatherhood with God's grace, they become tangible, accessible, and powerful examples that reveal profound truths about the heart of God. When we see how deeply, passionately, and sacrificially good fathers love their children, we can come to realize that these attributes are even more fully to be found in the heart of our heavenly Father.

Jesus himself used earthly fathers to reveal something of our heavenly Father. For example, in the Gospel of Matthew, Jesus says, "What man of you, if his son asks him for bread, will give him a stone? ... [H]ow much more will your Father who is in heaven give good things to those who ask him!" (Matthew 7:9, 11). While many fathers fall short of their calling to reflect the goodness of the heavenly Father, those shortcomings do not cancel God's plan to reveal himself through the lives of good fathers.

Understanding this is vitally important because the foundational question with which we wrestle is the identity of God. We see this in the Garden of Eden, where the temptation of Adam and Eve is essentially to doubt God's goodness. The Serpent entices them to doubt about whether or not God is acting for their good in forbidding them to eat of the Tree of the Knowledge of Good and Evil. All of us must wrestle with a similar temptation.

As the *Catechism of the Catholic Church* tells us, after the Fall "all subsequent sin would be disobedience toward God and lack of trust in his goodness" (CCC 397). The temptation to question God's care and goodness arises whenever his ways do not match up with ours; when his timeline does not match up with ours; and when the difficulties of life challenge us.

Knowing that we have a heavenly Father whose heart is infinitely good and loving changes everything. So, in this book, we are going to use stories and insights offered by earthly fatherhood to help us further understand and encounter the heart of our heavenly Father.

How This Book Works

To reflect on the goodness of God our Father and to draw us to his heart, each of the thirty meditations has two parts. First, we will tell the story of a father, either a biological or a spiritual father. Then we will reflect on a passage from Scripture, seeing the ways in which God himself has revealed these characteristics to be true of his own heart. Some of these passages are from the Old Testament, while others present the words and example of Jesus. As Philip requested of Jesus at the Last Supper, "Show us the Father, and we shall be satisfied." To which Jesus responds, "He who has seen me has seen the Father" (John 14:8–9). Our Lord reminds us that he is the divine Son of God and, as such, reveals the Father to us. All of Jesus' life, works, and teachings show us the character and heart of our good and gracious heavenly Father.

This book is meant to be a personal but guided retreat, a thirty-day reflection on the heart of God. As the Lord invited the people of Israel in the desert to gather manna on one day and not save some for the next, I would invite you to take a similar approach to reading this book. Be content to receive your daily bread by reading one meditation each day. The goal is not to finish reading this book quickly but to become ever more rooted in the life of God, to have his love and truth imprinted more deeply on your own heart.

It is a slow journey. We are looking for depth, not breadth. I encourage you to take it one day at a time and to read as early in the morning as possible. Then, throughout the rest of your day, reflect upon the specific characteristic of the Father's heart that the day's meditation revealed. Consider what this truth reveals to you about God and reveals to you about yourself. To help you in your reflection, each meditation is followed by space for you to write down your thoughts on the day's meditation.

My dear reader, I have been actively and passionately following the Lord as a disciple for the past twenty years, and I have been a Franciscan since 2009. One truth that I have come to experience deeply and passionately and that I want to shout from the rooftops is that our God is good, he is pursuing us, and he is the best of fathers. The Father is full of generosity, and he is worthy of our trust, our confidence, and our surrender. May the reading of this book be a source of grace, so that you too may encounter this truth.

Part 1
The Father's Delight in Us

1

THAT'S MY SON

At the age of twenty-one, Ronald Baptiste made a decision that would change the trajectory of his life and that of his future family. He saved up for months for a plane ticket, packed all he had into two little suitcases, and got on a flight from Haiti to the United States to begin a new life.

Going through the immigration process, he made his way up to New York, where he had a distant cousin. Slowly but surely, he learned his way around cars and got a job working at a car wash, where he eventually became a manager.

Because his coworkers were all Haitian and spoke Creole, Ronald never really became proficient in speaking English. Although his personality was naturally expressive and lively, he had become reserved and even shy when in situations where English was being spoken.

Ronald married and had two kids. One of his boys, Jean, became a baseball fan and Little League player. One Saturday afternoon, Ronald took Jean to the ballpark. As usual, Ronald found a seat in the bleachers and sat quietly, not comfortable enough with his command of English to engage the other parents.

Watching Jean play year after year, he had learned to appreciate the game. When Jean came up to bat on a particular Saturday afternoon, Ronald seemed calm but, as usual, he was a combination of excited and anxious.

On a 2–0 count, the pitcher grooved a fastball, and young Jean took a big, left-handed, Griffey-like swing and sent it deep over the right-field fence. Jean started running, rounding the bases for a home run, and as he turned the corner, he saw his dad standing up on his seat, shouting, "That's my son. That's my son. That's my son."

For Jean, the best part of that day, even more exciting than hitting a home run, was hearing his dad shouting, "That's my son." It was a memory that would remain with him for the rest of his life. He later became a priest, and it became a regular story in his homilies.

The story of Ronald shouting with pride, "That's my son. That's my son" can't help but make us recall the heavenly Father rending the heavens at the Jordan and breaking through the clouds on Mount Tabor. At Jesus' baptism and the Transfiguration, it is as if the Father could no longer withhold his pride and joy in his only begotten Son. The heavenly Father rends the heavens and shouts down, "This is my beloved Son. This is my beloved Son, listen to him."

God's Word

"And when Jesus was baptized, he went up immediately from the water, and behold, the heavens were opened and he saw the Spirit of God descending like a dove, and alighting on him; and behold, a voice from heaven, saying, 'This is my beloved Son, with whom I am well pleased'" (Matthew 3:16–17).

"Jesus took with him Peter and James and John and led them up a high mountain apart by themselves; and he was transfigured before them, and his garments became glistening, intensely white, as no fuller on earth could bleach them. And there appeared to them Elijah with Moses; and they were talking to Jesus ... And a cloud overshadowed them, and a voice came out of the cloud, 'This is my beloved Son; listen to him'" (Mark 9:2–4, 7).

What It Means for Us

At the great mystery of the Transfiguration, when the heavens are pulled back, we are given an insight into the eternal relationship between God the Father and God the Son, the first and second Persons of the Holy Trinity.

At the baptism of Jesus, the Father's voice was heard from heaven: "This is my beloved son with whom I am well pleased." When we were baptized, as the water was poured on our heads, the priest (or deacon) said, "I baptize you in the name of the Father, and of the Son, and of the Holy Spirit." At that moment, we were incorporated into Jesus' own relationship with his heavenly Father. We become his beloved children, with whom he is "well pleased."

Ronald's pride in his son was not limited to the day when he hit the home run. His pride in his son was constant, just as God the Father was always pleased with his Son, Jesus. We may not always feel like the heavens have been opened and these words are being spoken to us; nonetheless, this is how God the Father sees us.

St. Teresa of Calcutta (Mother Teresa) often spoke to her sisters about Jesus' thirst on the Cross. His thirst moved her and became a particular source of grace for her relationship with him, helping her experience his love for her. Mother Teresa told her sisters that, before everything else, we must experience Jesus' thirst for us in our hearts.

Similarly, before we can really know who we are and what the Lord is asking of us to do, we must experience the truth of these words: "You are my beloved son, you are my beloved daughter, with whom I am well pleased." In the quiet of our hearts, ask the Lord to speak these words in your life again today.

Let us pray.

Heavenly Father, my baptism and my faith tell me that I am your beloved son (daughter). Please speak these words in my life again today, especially in those areas where I struggle the most to experience that I am beloved in your eyes. We ask this in Jesus' name.

Amen.

A Place to Reflect

_____

_____

_____

_____

_____

_____

_____

_____

_____

_____

_____

_____

_____

_____

_____

_____

_____

_____

_____

_____

_____

_____

_____

_____

_____

2

THE BEST PART

Due to an emergency at the factory, Travis didn't get to bed until about 2:30 in the morning. As the plant manager, he had to stay late and make sure an order got shipped on time and that all the employees were safe.

When his alarm went off at 6:30 a.m., though, he got up without hesitation. As usual, he began his morning routine by checking on his twenty-five-year-old daughter, Angelle, who had cerebral palsy and was dependent on him and his wife.

He bent down, kissed her on the forehead, and said, "Angelle, it's time to get up." Her eyes opened, and she said, "Good morning, Dad." He picked her up and carried her into the bathroom to help her get ready for the day. Travis helped her use the restroom, helped her wash, got her dressed for the day, and then carried her downstairs and placed her in her wheelchair.

As they chatted, Travis made her some toast and poured her a glass of orange juice. After he got his own breakfast, he joined her at the table. Over the next hour or so, he helped her to eat her breakfast, then his wife came down and took over while he finished getting ready to go to work for the day.

That day, as he and his supervisor talked about what had happened the night before, his supervisor asked Travis if he had gotten any sleep. He said, "Sure, but I had my normal early morning routine." Travis then went on to describe a typical morning with his daughter. His supervisor replied, "Wow, that seems like a lot, like a real sacrifice. I don't know how you do it."

Travis looked at him and said, "No, you don't get it. My mornings with Angelle are the best part of my day."

Good fathers love to care for their children. From the outside looking in, this care might be perceived as a burden. To a loving father, though, it is not a burden but a blessing. In our relationship with our heavenly Father, we are invited to cast all our cares upon him, because he is the best of fathers and he cares for us (see 1 Peter 5:7).

God's Word

> "[God] found him in a desert land, and in the howling waste of the wilderness; he encircled him, he cared for him, he kept him as the apple of his eye" (Deuteronomy 32:10).

> "The LORD your God who goes before you will himself fight for you, just as he did for you in Egypt before your eyes, and in the wilderness, where you have seen how the LORD your God bore you, as a man bears his son" (Deuteronomy 1:30–31).

What It Means for Us

Throughout salvation history, God tells his people, in effect, "Come close. Come to me. Trust me. Give me your cares and let me care for you." Jesus says, "Come to me, all who labor and are heavy laden, and I will give you rest" (Matthew 11:28), and St. Peter in his first letter tells the first Christians, "Cast all your anxieties on him, for he cares about you" (1 Peter 5:7).

Certainly, we all have weaknesses and struggles. We all have incapacities and needs that can make us feel like we are a burden. Unfortunately, this insecurity is sometimes reinforced by spouses, parents, children, siblings, or coworkers by their words and attitudes toward us. But our heavenly

Father, wants us to surrender all to him, become wholly dependent on him, and allow him, in the small things and in the big things, to care for us and to carry us.

Travis took care of Angelle not because he *had* to as her father but because he *wanted* to. He saw helping her not as a burden or oppressive responsibility but truly as the best part of his day, year in and year out.

Let this truth that our heavenly Father desires to care for us permeate our hearts and let us trust in the Lord, bringing him our needs. It is not burdening him, but in fact, blessing the heart of our heavenly Father.

Let us pray.

Heavenly Father, so often I experience myself as a burden to myself, to those around me, and to you. Through the grace of the Holy Spirit, teach me to surrender to you, to trust you, to become dependent on you, and to cast all my cares upon you so that I can experience in the depths of my heart that you care for me. We ask this in Jesus' name.

Amen.

A Place to Reflect

3

CALLED BY NAME

Before Nick arrived at the homeless shelter, his "home" was the state penitentiary, where he had been confined for several years. Growing up in a broken family, Nick attempted to find a place in gangs, and the setting of his entire life could only be described as chaotic and dangerous.

Nick had been with us at the shelter for several months. He did not cause trouble, but he was somewhat reserved, even cold. This is often the effect of a violent background and years in prison. Such reserve is a way of warning others not to get too close.

We have dinner together at the shelter so that we might engage with the men, help them to express themselves, share some of their lives, and invite them to enter into friendship with us and each other. It is an opportunity to experience family. But Nick rarely opened up.

When someone enters the shelter, we ask for his date of birth. So, as a way of making the men feel more at home, we celebrate everyone's birthday with a cake. Nick's birthday was no exception. Though he had been present at birthday celebrations for other shelter residents, he doubted that we would remember his birthday.

After dinner that night, the lights in the dining hall were turned off as a couple of the friars and volunteers processed from the kitchen with a birthday cake with his name on it and decorated with candles. As the men joined in singing "Happy Birthday" to Nick, the friar on duty walked over and placed the cake in front of him.

But Nick did not blow out the candles. His head was bowed, with his chin resting on his chest. After several moments, someone turned the lights back on, and the friar who placed the cake in front of Nick got down on a knee and saw that Nick was crying. He put an arm on his shoulder and asked him if he was OK. Fighting back tears, Nick looked at the friar and said, "It's just that I have never had a birthday cake with my name on it."

This might have been the first time in his life that Nick had felt celebrated and loved, as he saw his name written on a birthday cake in a homeless shelter.

God's Word

> "Now thus says the LORD, he who created you, O Jacob, he who formed you, O Israel: 'Fear not, for I have redeemed you; I have called you by name, you are mine'" (Isaiah 43:1).

What It Means for Us

As the book of Isaiah tells us, "I have called you by name, you are mine." Names play an important role in our lives; in fact, they can define how we experience life. When someone knows our name—and calls us by it—this shows that they know us as a unique person. All of us desire to be known by name, to be called by name, and to be loved by name. This desire is something that God has planted in our hearts, for he has created us by name. In other words, he created us with particular and unique attention.

As the psalmist writes, "You knitted me together in my mother's womb" (Psalm 139:13). God knows us intimately. He knows us by name. The power of his personal knowledge of each of us is reflected in Jesus' calling of Nathaniel. When Philip finds Nathaniel under a fig tree and brings him to Jesus, the Lord tells him, "Before Philip called you, when you were under the fig tree, I saw you" (John 1:48). So Jesus saw him, knew him, and loved him. When Jesus calls each of the apostles, he calls them by name—and some he even gives new names. By calling them by name, Jesus communicates that he sees them, and he knows them.

In the noise of everyday life, in the traffic and busyness of so many people around us, we can be tempted to feel like we are just another face in the crowd and that nobody would notice if we were gone. We wrestle with such questions as, *Does anyone care? Do I matter to anyone?* The answer is yes.

There is something so beautiful about being called by name and celebrated by name. There is something moving about hearing somebody with authority or prestige call us by name. It is powerful to realize that a person who knows many people and is respected by many still knows us and cares about us. How much more profoundly can we experience and receive this gift as God the Father knows us by name?

Perhaps this is why the Lord has communicated again and again, both in word and action, throughout the Scriptures and salvation history, the words of the prophet Isaiah: "I have called you by name, you are mine." Each of us is known and loved by God our Father.

Please consider taking a moment in prayer today to sit intentionally before your heavenly Father. Allow him to look upon you, to celebrate you, and to call you by name.

Let us pray.

Heavenly Father, may we experience again the truth and depth of this love that you call us by name and that we are yours. May we find rest and peace and the affirmation we so desire in you as you call us by name again this day. We ask this in Jesus' name.

Amen.

A Place to Reflect

4

CRY OUT, "ABBA! FATHER!"

Asis had just wrapped up a forty-eight-hour shift on Thursday and Friday down at the firehouse where he worked. As any man would be, he was physically tired out after being on duty for so long. Unlike most men, though, Asis was still on duty when he went home because an emergency could happen at any moment. He was going home to care for his two-year-old son, John Paul, who had a feeding tube.

John Paul was born with a genetic condition that left him fragile and vulnerable, and Asis and his wife, Michelle, knew that the fact that he had already made it to two years of life was a miracle. Every day was a gift.

The gift of John Paul's life was something Asis and Michelle never took for granted. It was a gift he cherished every day because John Paul was their fourth child, but he was the only one who had not made the journey yet to eternal life. Their other three children shared the same genetic condition. They lost their first, Providence, through a miscarriage. Their second child, Asis Gabriel, named after his father and grandfather, continued his pilgrimage to the Father's house when he was just a few weeks old. Asis and Michelle then conceived a third child, a daughter named Piera, whose earthly life ended in the womb at six months old.

As they received the gift of each child's life in turn and were asked to give that gift back to God so soon, the hearts of Asis and Michelle were wrenched with suffering. With a strength that only God could give, they welcomed each child and walked with each of their children for his or her short time of pilgrimage in this life. With each loss, they were bleeding and being poured out, sharing in the suffering of Jesus' own wounded side. But they welcomed their children with open hearts.

When Asis' first son Gabriel was born, he and Michelle received him as one sent with a mission. They took it upon themselves to be totally available and supportive during his short time on earth. For Asis, there was nothing that made him happier than watching his friends and family members hold Gabriel, look at him, and love him—and be looked upon and loved by him. During the few weeks of his son's life, Asis would stand beside his son, in contemplation, as friends and family held Gabriel and gazed at him.

After Gabriel's passing, the doctors told Asis and Michelle that there was a medical way they could avoid passing the genetic condition on to future children, but the proposed method violated the sanctity of human life. Asis told the doctor, "God can send me a hundred children like this. I'll take each and every one."

When Michelle became pregnant with their third child, Piera, she and Asis were told that early tests indicated that she would never be born. The pain was great, and the temptation was to protect themselves from having their hearts broken again.

Asis prayed for the grace to fully accept the gift of his daughter. One night, he knelt, placed his ear on his wife's womb, and heard his daughter—and claimed her as his own. He gave Piera access to his whole heart, no matter the cost. At six months in the womb, Piera's earthly pilgrimage ended, and Asis experienced again the pain that comes from the loss of a child. But he did not regret a single moment of loving and being a father to Piera and to all his children. He had resolved to give the fullness of his heart to any children, regardless of their medical condition, that God gave him and his wife.

When John Paul was born and diagnosed with the same condition, Asis and Michelle knew what to expect. John Paul spent the first seven weeks of his life in the NICU, and when he came home, he was totally and completely dependent on care, needing oxygen and feeding tubes. For Asis, one of his great joys was that John Paul was able to recognize his parents' faces and could smile or laugh when they saw him. His life was beautiful but fragile.

As John Paul grew, Michelle and Asis brought him with them to Mass and wherever they went. They desired to share the gift of their son with the world. He even became a bit of a local celebrity. Through his little ways, he found a place—a privileged place—in the hearts of many.

Asis and Michelle experienced much emotion in the challenges and joys that went with their unique journey of parenthood. One of the most moving experiences of fatherhood for Asis was taking little John Paul to church. At some point, somebody would always recognize Asis and say, "Oh, you're John Paul's father." In recounting this, Asis was moved to tears. He said that to be John Paul's father was enough. Just being his dad was enough; it was all he wanted.

In the relationship Asis had with John Paul, we have a reflection of the deep love of God the Father for us, his children. St. Paul in his letter to the Romans tells us that we call God by the name "Father." He loves being our Father.

God's Word

"You have received the spirit of sonship. When we cry, 'Abba! Father!'
it is the Spirit himself bearing witness with our spirit that we are
children of God" (Romans 8:15–16).

What It Means for Us

John Paul was entirely dependent, unable to speak with words, but he spoke profoundly with his life. Simply by his life, he gave his father the greatest title, the greatest name, and the greatest way of being known—as John Paul's dad. For Asis, that was enough; it was everything.

The Son of God, the second Person of the Trinity, received a human name—Jesus—when he became flesh for us. Jesus teaches us to call upon God the Father, his Father, as "Our Father." It is the Holy Spirit within us that cries out, "Abba! Father!" From all eternity, this is who God the Father *is*—he is *Father*. In communicating his name to us in this way, he tells us that being Father is the fullness of who he is.

Since there are more than eight billion people on earth, we can be tempted to focus on our own littleness and think that we are too insignificant for God to care about us. We do not want to "waste his time" with our little concerns, needs, frustrations, or joys. Perhaps we experience our weaknesses and limitations and feel like this is a reason for removing ourselves from a relationship with God the Father. But there are few things that hurt us—and the heart of God the Father—more than when we live in this way.

In Baptism, we come to share in Jesus' relationship with his Father, so we truly have the right to call God "Father." So, we can announce to the whole world that God is our Father. Calling him Father is the greatest expression of gratitude we can give him because, in his great love for us, his children, he rejoices in this name.

Asis said that being—and being known as—John Paul's dad was his greatest joy, his greatest gift, and his greatest treasure. Similarly, the greatest joy of God the Father is to be *my* father, to be *your* father, and to be *our* Father, as all of us share in the Sonship of Jesus through our baptism.

Living from this place, let us without hesitation or reservation cry out to God the Father, call him Father, and allow him to be Father to us. Let us with our lives, words, and all that we are proclaim to the world the good news that we have a Father in heaven—and that he rejoices in his Fatherhood.

Let us pray.

Heavenly Father, we thank you for the gift of your name. We thank you for this relationship and the way you see us and rejoice in us and glory in being our Father. May we live from this place and receive the gift that you offer us, the sweetness of your name upon our lips. We make this prayer in the name of Jesus the Lord.

Amen.

A Place to Reflect

5

WONDERFULLY MADE

It had been a long forty-eight hours for Tom. Needless to say, it had been an even longer forty-eight hours for his wife, Joanna. On Monday night, they had gone to the hospital for the birth of their first child, Benedict. After a long period of labor and some time needed for extra observation, mom, dad, and baby headed back to their Long Island apartment late on Wednesday night.

As soon as they got home, Tom helped Joanna lie down so that she could get some much-needed rest and begin her own recovery from so many long hours of labor, including some complications. Then Tom went over to Benedict's crib, picked him up, and held him. Although he had not slept for two days, there was no way he was going to sleep anytime soon as he held his newborn son.

All night, Tom stayed awake holding Benedict, taking in his little nose and cheeks, and listening with excitement to his little breaths and snores. His own heart was beating with each breath his infant son took.

Hour after hour after hour, Tom just held him and stared at him. He smiled. He cried. He prayed. He was radically overcome in contemplation of the most beautiful, majestic, awesome sight he had ever beheld, his newborn son.

If an earthly father can know how beautifully and wonderfully we are made, how much more can our heavenly Father.

God's Word

> *"God created man in his own image, in the image of God he created him;*
> *male and female he created them ... And God saw everything that*
> *he had made, and behold, it was very good"* (Genesis 1:27, 31).

> *"Even the hairs of your head are all numbered"* (Matthew 10:30).

What It Means for Us

In the beginning, God created the heavens and the earth. He filled the sky. He molded the mountains. He dug the oceans. Creation is majestic and awesome; it is called "good." But it was not until God created man that the Scriptures use the words "*very* good." There is a unique dignity, beauty, and goodness to us, God's children.

When Tom held his newborn son, he was rapt with wonder just looking at him. An earthly father comes to know his son not by infused knowledge but by gazing at him. I think this image helps us understand the way our heavenly Father knows us. He is always looking at us. His heart is moved by all the little nuances, particularities, and intricacies of the personality and the face of each of us, his unique son or daughter.

Our Lord tells us that all of our hairs are counted (see Luke 12:7), not just that they are known. This is a great reminder of the tremendous and tender love that our heavenly Father has for us. He never takes his eyes off us.

A human father has a limited capacity to contemplate his children. But our heavenly Father can look at each of us eternally. God the Father constantly looks upon us as if we were his firstborn. It is this God who knows us intimately, who is the author of our life, who instructs us, who teaches us, and who shepherds us.

Our heavenly Father knows us—and he loves us. May our understanding of this truth lead us to a profound trust in him. As life happens and we don't always know why this or that thing is happening or where we are going, let us be renewed in this confidence, trusting that all of the hairs on our head are counted. The One who is leading us knows us and loves us—and his eyes are always upon us.

Let us pray.

Heavenly Father, I believe that I am beautifully and wonderfully made. I trust that you look upon me and that you see me and that you believe that I am very good. I believe, Lord, that you know me, intricately and intimately, and that you love me. May this be the source of my trust in you as you continue to lead me deeper into the mysteries of your divine life through the mysteries of this passing earthly life. We ask this in the name of Jesus.

Amen.

A Place to Reflect

6

ALL SHE HAD

When the Franciscan Friars of the Renewal were first established back in 1987 in the South Bronx, their house was in a pretty rough neighborhood. It had a reputation for drug use, gangs, burned-out cars, and violence. In those early days, many of the people the friars ministered to were living in the rawness of this troubled area.

One of our dear friends and neighbors who would be a part of the friars' broader family for decades to come was a woman named Araceli. She had kind of "seen it all" and "done it all." She had suffered all sorts of trauma, including her own addiction and bouts with violence.

Through a relationship with the friars and the sisters, she slowly began to have a conversion and began to take her faith seriously. But the rough edges of one's humanity do not get smoothed out overnight. Conversion from past wounds takes time. This was true in Araceli's case. We loved her, but she was still on the journey of healing as we all are.

As a result of her background, Araceli had multiple piercings on her face. The brothers knew that she had experienced a lot of pain in her life, and they deeply wanted her to be at peace. Since Araceli's piercings were something that had come from a time of woundedness, some of the brothers would lovingly encourage her to remove them simply as a way to live in the fullness of her new life.

One Saturday, at about eight o'clock in the morning, Araceli arrived at the friary. On that particular Saturday, some of the friars were being ordained priests at St. Patrick's Cathedral in Manhattan. Araceli asked to come along because she wanted to celebrate this day with them, the community, and the Church.

So Araceli joined us as we were finishing up a quick breakfast and getting our things together to leave for the ordinations. In her own Bronx way, Araceli said, "Hey, brothers. Do you see what I did? Somebody say something." We all looked at her and immediately noticed that she had removed all of her facial piercings. It was a little gift that she wanted to give as a way for her to celebrate the brothers. She said, "See, brothers, for you guys I took out the piercings for today."

For the brothers, there was something about this little gesture of Araceli that made it a profound treasure and gift to them. They recognized that this was the most that she could give, and they saw the sincerity with which she gave it. Though most people would say it was a small gesture, to the brothers it was deeply moving. She loved us and showed her love the best she could.

God's ways are not our ways (see Isaiah 55:8–9). How he sees us and how he judges are not how we see and how we judge. Jesus, who reveals the Father to us, shows us this when he pointed out to the apostles that the offering of the poor widow, two small coins, was greater than those of the rich because she gave all she had, from her heart.

God's Word

"He looked up and saw the rich putting their gifts into the treasury;
and he saw a poor widow put in two copper coins. And he said,
'Truly I tell you, this poor widow has put in more than all of them;

*for they all contributed out of their abundance, but she out of her
poverty put in all the living that she had'" (Luke 21:1–4).*

What It Means for Us

This poor widow must have suffered much because she had nothing left
but her two coins. But she gave them as a gift. In the grand scheme of
things, it wasn't a big help to the capital campaign, yet it is what Jesus
highlights as the most profound and beautiful gift. God does not see the
way we see. Rather, he sees this offering as the greatest treasure because
this poor widow gave everything she had.

Wasn't this the case with Araceli? She gave what she could. In her
situation, the gift that she could give was taking out her piercings as a sign
of love for her brothers. As a community dependent on divine Providence
manifested through the generosity of many donors, we have been the
recipient of many large financial gifts. Yet, to us, there remains something
even more moving and beautiful about Araceli's gesture. The Temple had
the widow's coins; we had the widow's multiple nose and lip piercings.

For many of us, life has been difficult, and it has left us unable to give
the fullness of what we think we should be able to give. Perhaps we want
to volunteer more, be more generous with our charitable contributions,
pray more, be kinder and more patient, or be better mothers, fathers,
disciples, or evangelists. But we experience our poverty again and again in
the frustration and disappointment of not being able to give as we desire.
Often, we find ourselves not being able to give very much at all. But God
doesn't see things the way we see them.

We know the Lord's invitation. He calls us to love him with all our heart,
strength, and mind. Notice that this is a call to love with the strength *we*
have, not the strength an *ideal person* might have or the strength we think
we *should* have. God calls us to give what we can, as much as we can, even
if this is just a "few coins." For Araceli, it was her piercings. What we can
give might be a little more trust, or a little more time. What we can give

might be just a little more confidence in the Lord's ability to provide where we cannot provide for ourselves.

For our heavenly Father, what matters is not the gift given but the love with which it is given. Perhaps it is a small gift. Perhaps the gift is just a cry for help. But if it is done with love and sincerity, we can have confidence that it is truly an offering pleasing to the heart of our Father.

Let us pray.

Heavenly Father, we experience our own poverty and frustration, especially in our inability to love you as we know you should be loved, to serve you as we know you should be served, and to give ourselves in the way we really think we should be able to give ourselves. May we find rest by recognizing that you do not judge us as we judge ourselves, but that you see the heart. Help us to recognize that you receive with great joy and gratitude our poor little gifts of love. We ask this in Jesus' name.

Amen.

A Place to Reflect

_____

_____

_____

_____

_____

_____

_____

_____

_____

_____

_____

_____

_____

7

TELLING EVERYONE

There he was, doing it again, and the extended McGann family laughed and rolled their eyes. For what seemed to be the sixth or seventh time, Mr. McGann was telling some random person in Manhattan about his son Eddie, the police officer.

Every year, the McGann family has a tradition of going into the city at Christmas time to see all the decorations. Year after year, they have become accustomed to the tradition of Mr. McGann telling anybody who would listen about his son Eddie, the police officer. When he saw police officers, he would tell them; at the restaurant, he would tell the server; and the Uber driver would hear about it as well.

The McGann family finds this particularly amusing because Eddie is not a new police officer; he has been on the force for nearly ten years. Still, whenever Mr. McGann gets the chance, whether he is in the city, talking to his car mechanic, or waiting in line at the store, he loves to tell everybody that his son Eddie is a police officer.

When his family teases him, "Dad, you can't keep telling everybody about Eddie," he says, "Well, I'm so proud of him, and I love to tell everybody about it. I'm his dad, and that's my right."

A father loves to talk about his children. In the Gospel of John, as his Passion approaches, Jesus speaks to his Father about his disciples, who are also children of the Father.

God's Word

> *"Father, I desire that they also, whom you have given me, may be with me where I am, to behold my glory which you have given me in your love for me before the foundation of the world. O righteous Father, the world has not known you, but I have known you; and these know that you have sent me. I made known to them your name, and I will make it known, that the love with which you have loved me may be in them, and I in them"* (John 17:24–26).

What It Means for Us

There are only a few times in the New Testament where the veil is pierced, and we get insight into Jesus' relationship with his Father. In the Gospel of John, we are brought into this mystery as he communicates with the Father directly in what is known as Jesus' high priestly prayer.

In this prayer, we hear him speak to his heavenly Father about his disciples, basically saying that they are the Father's gift to him. His disciples, of course, were not perfect. They had their limitations, weaknesses, and struggles. They had their petty arguments and squabbles. But still, they were gifts from the Father—and Jesus received them as gifts.

Jesus' high priestly prayer is an insight into the ongoing dialogue within the Most Holy Trinity. The heavenly Father loves to speak of his children. For all eternity, there is an ongoing and total gift of the Father, Son, and Holy Spirit to one another. Mysteriously and mystically tied to this Trinitarian love are you and me. Perhaps speaking a bit poetically, it could be said that this giving thanks to the Father for the gift of his disciples is included as the eternal conversation in the life of the Trinity. The three divine Persons are continually celebrating each of us as a gift. If an earthly father never tires of talking about his children, how much more could this be said of our heavenly Father?

If a father like Mr. McGann cannot help but tell everyone about how proud he is of his son, the police officer, how much more can our heavenly Father never cease to share how proud he is of each of us. Perhaps we can imagine the Father holding court with all the angels and the saints, telling them about us, about you and me, rejoicing in our successes and pointing out our individual particularities. At this very moment, you are being given, received, and spoken about by the Most Holy Trinity as a beloved gift.

Let us pray.

Heavenly Father, how often our interior dialogue is one of criticism and negativity; how often we are tempted to wonder if we are good, if we matter. May we know and be renewed in knowing that you love us and that you see us as a gift, and that, like the best of fathers, you never tire of speaking of and boasting about us as your beloved children. We ask this in Jesus' name.

Amen.

A Place to Reflect

_____

_____

_____

_____

_____

_____

_____

_____

_____

8

BEAUTIFUL IN HIS EYES

Claire and Bryce were getting closer to their wedding day. As part of their wedding preparation, they talked about the kind of parents they wanted to be and how they could learn from the example of their own parents, both positive and negative. For Claire, conversations with Bryce about her father were difficult because, in many ways, he struggled to communicate his love for her in the way Claire needed. Her father wound was painful.

In one conversation, Bryce asked Claire, "Is there any situation where you really felt loved by your dad? Did you ever feel like he did a good job caring for you?" When Claire thought about it, one memory that came to mind was when she was eleven. As every parent knows, children can struggle in school if they are different in any way. As an eleven-year-old, Claire had curly hair and was taller than all the kids in her class, so she often got teased. For several weeks, she would come home and cry every day after school, and she begged her parents to be homeschooled.

At those moments, when he got home from work, her father would go and talk to her and hear her out. Again and again, he told her, "I love you just the way you are. I wouldn't change anything about you. You're beautiful. The other kids don't know what they're doing, and they will learn. But I love you, and I wouldn't change a thing about you." But he also had a "tough love" approach, saying, "You are not going to change schools. You are going to learn from this and grow; you are not going to run from your struggles. You will get through this." At the end of his talks with Claire, he would look intently at her and say again, "Claire, I need you to listen to me. You're beautiful, and I love you, and I wouldn't change anything about you."

As an adult reflecting back on that time in her life, Claire admits that, yes, she heard her father's words, but she didn't really receive them. She dismissed them because she thought, *Well, that's just what dads have to say.* She didn't really believe him.

With the support of her mom and dad, Claire kept going to the same school. Eventually, the other kids caught up to her, and being different was no longer seen as being a bad thing. Still, even at twenty, she struggled because she had never really received the words of her father: "You're beautiful, and I love you, and I wouldn't change a thing about you."

We can consider Claire's story and think about the way we respond to our heavenly Father. We can think of the story of the hemorrhaging woman, who came to Jesus to be healed but tried to keep him from seeing her.

God's Word

> "A woman who had had a flow of blood for twelve years and had spent all her living upon physicians and could not be healed by any one, came up behind him, and touched the fringe of his garment; and immediately her flow of blood ceased. And Jesus said, 'Who was it that touched me?' When all denied it … Jesus said, 'Some one touched me, for I perceive that power has gone forth from me.' And when the woman saw that she was not hidden, she came trembling, and falling down before him declared in the presence of all the people why she had touched him, and how she had been immediately healed. And he said to her, 'Daughter, your faith has made you well; go in peace'" (Luke 8:43–48).

What It Means for Us

This woman had become an outcast because of her suffering. Then she heard about Jesus. When she approached Jesus to touch the tassel of his cloak, believing that it could save her and heal her, she did so from behind. The Gospel tells us that she came not wanting to be seen, and as soon as she touched the tassel of Jesus and was healed, she immediately faded into the background and hid again. This is a profound detail of the story.

Jesus then stops everything and causes a scene, asking, "Who touched me?" The woman who had been healed then came forward, apologizing as if she had done something wrong. We can imagine how she looked, downcast at first, then raising her eyes to meet those of Jesus. Instead of hearing words of rebuke, she saw in his face the truth: "I love you. I know you. I want you. I'm seeking you. You are good." This truth is summed up in Jesus' first word to her—"daughter." Here, we see how Jesus reveals the Father to us, in this woman who encounters the face of Jesus, now knowing that she is a beloved daughter of God. Now she could be truly healed and could go in peace.

How difficult it is for us to believe the Lord's own words and actions, to look at ourselves the way he looks at us. He comes seeking us, asking us to come to him and pray so that we can receive the truth of who we are in his eyes. There are so many other voices and so many experiences condemning us and telling us we are not good enough. The difficulty is these voices become the ones we listen to and end up forming how we see ourselves.

We see this reality echoed in Claire's story. Isn't this what so many of us experience as we read the Scriptures, sit in prayer, or look at a crucifix? From the crucifix, the Lord says to us, "I know you, I love you, I desire to be with you forever." Our heavenly Father proclaims his love for us—a love with which pursues us, even to the point of sending his Son to die for us and save us, because he wants us to be with him forever. God proclaims that he knit each of us together in our mother's womb, and that we are beautifully and wonderfully made (see Psalm 139:13–14). He proclaims his particular love for each of us. But how much do we struggle to really receive it?

Let us turn to God, the Father, Son, and Holy Spirit, and know that he loves us, looks upon us, and knows us—and that we truly are good and beautiful in his eyes. When he says that he loves us, let's believe him!

Let us pray.

Heavenly Father, you say that I am good and that you love me, but I struggle to believe it. I struggle not to dismiss it as an abstraction—as some generality spoken to the crowd. Grant me the grace to come to you in prayer, to behold your face. Help me to sit with your Word, to come before your presence in the Most Holy Eucharist, to look at your love proclaimed on the crucifix. And from you, Lord, may I be open to receiving the truth that I am beloved.

Amen.

A Place to Reflect

9

BE WITH HIM

At seven o'clock on the Monday morning after Thanksgiving in the teachers' lounge at Memorial High School, there was heavy foot traffic around the coffee machine, as usual.

Jacob arrived, grabbed himself a coffee, then dropped his bags on the table next to his longtime mentor, Charlie, and pulled up a chair. Immediately, Jacob jumped into an excited retelling of his long weekend with his kids. Charlie, twenty years older than Jacob, did what he normally did—he listened. Jacob's two kids, Pearl and Elijah, were at the "fun ages" of four and six.

"It couldn't have been a better Thanksgiving break," Jacob told Charlie, with all the loud enthusiasm of a young dad. "Friday night we watched *Aladdin* again and ate popcorn, we snuggled on the couch, then I told Pearl and Elijah a story. They get so excited as I tell it to them. Then I put them to bed and watched them sleep for a bit.

"Then, on Saturday, we went to the park and worked on riding bikes. Pearl is still a little afraid, but Elijah has no fear in the world. After that, we had a picnic, then went home, had dinner, and played some games.

"I just love being a dad so much. And my kids kind of smother me and follow me around the house. Maybe I should want some space, but to be honest, I love how much they want to be around me. Though I have only been a dad for a few years, it really is the best thing in the world."

As Charlie listened to Jacob rave about the joys of being a dad, he was smiling but inside he couldn't help but feel his own pain. Charlie's kids were now in their late teens and twenties, and he was heartbroken because, for Thanksgiving, one of his daughters chose to stay at school, his older son chose to celebrate with his girlfriend's family, and his teenage son barely came out of his room the entire day.

While Charlie was normally good at sharing in the joys of his young, excited teacher friend, he couldn't restrain words he could usually keep himself from saying. He said, "Jacob, savor every moment of this, because someday your kids will grow up, and they are not going to make time for you. And it really hurts."

Is there anything a father wants to do more than spend time with his children? To look at them, love them, and have that love reciprocated? To know that his kids love him as their father?

When Jesus called the apostles, the Gospel says he called them to be with him. Jesus, image of the Father, deeply desired to be with them—and in that calling we learn something about our heavenly Father.

God's Word

> "And he went up into the hills, and called to him those whom he desired; and they came to him. And he appointed twelve, to be with him, and to be sent out to preach" (Mark 3:13–14).

What It Means for Us

Jesus came to save us. He came to form us, to teach us and to have us learn from him. But first and foremost, he calls us to be with him. Being with Jesus was formative for the disciples, and it was a way in which he communicated his divine life to them.

In addition, we can understand that Jesus, who reveals the Father to us, just deeply desired to be with his disciples in his humanity. And surely his heart was filled as they came to him and enjoyed his company. Certainly, there was an experience of human sadness when they didn't come to him, when they didn't turn to him for help, when they didn't seek him, and when they tried to do things on their own.

Our heavenly Father deeply desires to spend time with us. Although we go through different phases in our spiritual lives, we always need to make time for him. We could visit with him in the chapel to tell him we love him and are thankful for his presence in our lives or participate in the Holy Sacrifice of the Mass. We could spend time in the morning listening to him and telling him our hopes, sorrows, and joys. We could take time in the evening to thank him for the day. Let us make time in our day to tell God the Father that we are grateful for his fatherhood and that we love him.

Our Father in heaven deeply desires for us to remain near to him. May we respond to this cry of all fathers' hearts and the cry of the heart of our heavenly Father to have us, his children, remain close to him every day.

Let us pray.

Heavenly Father, I love you, and I know that you love me. But I know that you love me with a love that is greater than my understanding. I am sorry for all the times I have failed to make time for you, to remain close to you. Fill me with the grace of the Holy Spirit so that I may begin anew. Help me to be generous in making time to be with you, to tell you that I love you and that I am grateful for your fatherhood in my life.

Amen.

A Place to Reflect

_____
_____
_____
_____
_____
_____
_____
_____
_____
_____
_____
_____
_____
_____
_____
_____
_____
_____
_____
_____
_____
_____
_____
_____
_____
_____
_____
_____
_____
_____

10

WITHOUT COUNTING THE COST

When Daniella, the oldest of four, went off to college, she was excited but soon became homesick. She chose to attend a school more than two hours away from home. Since Daniella was close to her family, she would call her parents nearly every day to check in and see how things were going at home.

At three o'clock one day, Daniella's dad, José, gave her a call to check in and see how she was doing. Talking to Daniella that day broke his heart. She shared that she was feeling overwhelmed with studying. She had a big exam the next day, and she was really anxious about it. She also spoke about some drama with some of her friends, and she ended the call in tears, saying how alone and sad she felt.

Immediately after getting off the phone with his daughter, José called his wife, Angelica. He told her about Daniella's struggles and said that he was going to drive over to the college to see her.

José then got in touch with his supervisor, telling him that he would need to take off a couple of hours early. Since he had always been a diligent employee, his boss said it was no problem.

José began the drive to Daniella's college. As he got close to the campus, he pulled into a gift shop and bought her some of her favorite cookies, some flowers, and a little stuffed panda bear, her favorite animal since her childhood. Daniella heard knocking on her door. When she opened it, she saw her dad standing there with the flowers, cookies, and teddy bear, and she immediately jumped into his arms.

At the door, José held his daughter close as she cried in his arms. He said, "Daniella, I just want you to know I'm so proud of you, and that I love you so much. I know you're stressed out and that you have to study, so I'm not going to take up much of your time. But I just wanted to come. I want you to know that I'm always here for you, that I'm always thinking about you, that I'm always proud of you, and I love you so much."

After a few more minutes, Daniella found some peace. They picked up the flowers, cookies, and panda bear off the ground. Her father hugged her one more time and said, "If you ever need anything, you know your mom and I are always here for you. I love you." He closed the door and drove home.

José drove for more than four hours that day to spend less than five minutes with his daughter. But they are five minutes Daniella will remember for the rest of her life.

As we see this abundant love in José's story, we can think of our heavenly Father, who loves abundantly. There is a gratuitousness to God's fatherhood. Look at the gifts he gives, from the creation of the world to the ultimate gift of his only begotten Son.

God's Word

"In the beginning God created the heavens and earth ... And God said, 'Let the earth put forth vegetation, plants yielding seed, and fruit trees bearing fruit in which is their seed, each according to its kind' ... And God said, 'Let there be lights in the firmament of the heavens' ... And God said, 'Let the water bring forth swarms

of living creatures, and let birds fly above the earth across the firmament of the heavens' ... And God said, 'Let the earth bring forth living creatures according to their kinds'" (Genesis 1:1, 11, 14, 20, 24).

"For God so loved the world that he gave his only-begotten Son, that whoever believes in him should not perish but have eternal life" (John 3:16).

What It Means for Us

Consider the whole of creation: the stars, the depths of the ocean, and the intricacies of each atom and cell. In his love, God creates lavishly, even seemingly excessively. He is not frugal with his love; he gives it abundantly.

In the fullness of time, the Lord came to seek us and save us. Certainly, God the Father could have saved us in a different, easier way than by sending his only begotten Son to become man, crawl among us as a baby, walk with us as a man, and be betrayed and crucified as a Savior. He did not need to do all this to save us, but he did so out of the abundance of his love.

Let's look to the Cross, the instrument of our "re-creation." On the Cross, we encounter a love without measure. Also, as we receive the gift of Jesus' Body, Blood, Soul, and Divinity in the Holy Eucharist, may we see the abundant love that God has for us. He never ceases to give himself totally to us. He holds back nothing. May we hold back nothing from him.

For a father's love, there is nothing too excessive or abundant when it comes to loving his children. As recipients of so lavish a love, may we give as we have received and so imitate what we contemplate.

Let us pray.

Heavenly Father, thank you for the abundance of your love, the lavishness of your love. Help me to receive this gift and to know that I'm never alone. Help me to know how deeply you desire my good, my peace, and my response to this love. Show me how to without counting the cost. Help me to be magnanimous in pouring my life out in mercy and generosity to my brothers and sisters, especially those most in need. We ask this is Jesus' name.

Amen.

A Place to Reflect

_____

_____

_____

_____

_____

_____

_____

_____

_____

_____

_____

_____

_____

_____

_____

_____

_____

_____

_____

_____

_____

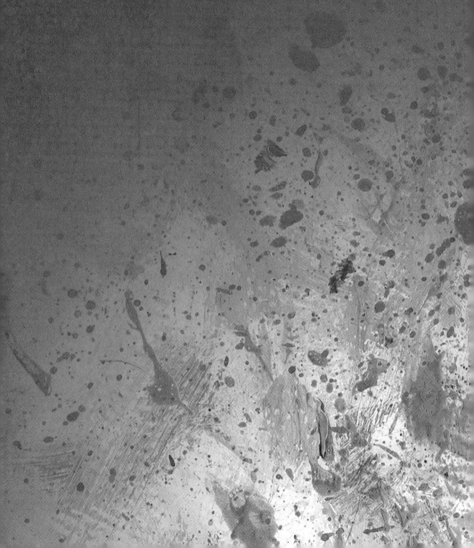

Part 2

The Father's Care for Us

11

HE LOVED TO THE END

Ryan's diagnosis came out of nowhere. He was a father of five in his late forties, seemingly in good health. When he began to experience symptoms he couldn't explain, he went to a doctor to get a check-up. After some tests, the news from the doctor was basically a worst-case scenario. He had stage four, inoperable cancer that had become already extremely invasive, but it was treatable.

Ryan shared this difficult news with his wife and children and extended family, and they all began to pray for him as he began treatment. A prayer chain went out, and hundreds of people began praying for Ryan and his health, as they were moved by the story of a young father with such a grave diagnosis.

Although Ryan found the treatment hard to tolerate, he suffered through it so that he might be around for his family. Sadly, a few months later the treatment was no longer effective, and Ryan found himself in the hospital. Although he was dying and in great pain, he connected with a family lawyer and spent his final days making sure that his wife and kids were going to be taken care of.

With the help of the lawyer, he set up a trust fund for his children and arranged that each year on their birthdays a card and a certain amount of money would be given to them for their needs. This ongoing gift from a father to his children was an expression of his love and desire to continue to provide and care for them after his passing. This was one of Ryan's final acts, as his cancer had begun shutting down his organs and he soon passed away.

In some ways, it is not surprising that a father would use his last moments to care for and provide for his children. This speaks to the beauty and dignity of fatherhood. A father's life, heart, and concerns are no longer his own but are for his wife and children.

Similarly, this gives us an important insight into the final days of Jesus' life on earth, as well as how he continues to provide for us and care for us, revealing to us the heart of the Father.

God's Word

> *"When Jesus knew that his hour had come to depart out of this world to the Father, having loved his own who were in the world, he loved them to the end" (John 13:1–5).*

> *"The Lord Jesus on the night when he was betrayed took bread, and when he had given thanks, he broke it, and said, 'This is my body which is for you. Do this in remembrance of me'" (1 Corinthians 11:23–24).*

> *"When Jesus saw his mother, and the disciple whom he loved standing near [the cross], he said to his mother, 'Woman, behold, your son!' Then he said to the disciple, 'Behold, your mother!'" (John 19:26–27).*

What It Means for Us

On the night before Jesus was betrayed, he celebrated the Last Supper with his apostles and gave us his own Body and Blood in the Holy Eucharist.

While hanging on the Cross, he breathed out the words, "Father, forgive them; for they know not what they do" (Luke 23:34). He offered salvation to the good thief dying beside him (see Luke 23:43). And then looking at the beloved disciple, and seeing in him all of us, he said, "Behold, your mother."

In his final moments, he still thought of us. He loved us until the end. One expression of his love for us was providing a way to receive his love on our journey. What did he give us? He gave us the gift of his very self, Emmanuel, in the Most Blessed Sacrament. He gave us his Body, Blood, Soul, and Divinity so that we can always come to him and remain close to him. He gave us himself so that he can always come and enter our very souls, strengthening us and loving us, uniting us to himself from within.

In addition, he gave us the gift of his mother, the Blessed Virgin Mary, whose love, tenderness, strength, and guidance he had personally experienced during his earthly life. So Jesus, in a special act of love in his final moments on earth, gave us his mother to love us, guide us, and strengthen us, and to care for us on the journey through life, as she did for Jesus. As a mother, she gives us the gift of peace that comes from trusting God in all circumstances with tenderness and strength.

As they receive their birthday gift every year, Ryan's children are reminded of his particular love and providence for them as their father. They remember that they were the focus of his final energy and effort on earth.

At every moment when we pray to Mary as our mother, go to Eucharistic Adoration, or participate in the sacrifice of the Mass, may we truly remember that, just as Ryan loved his children in his final moments, so does Jesus love us. He loved us to the end. But he continues to love us with a love that does not end. He remains our strength for the journey.

Let us pray.

Heavenly Father, we know that you love us. In Jesus, you love us
to the end. You love us in a way that provides for us and cares for

us, particularly through the gifts of the Most Holy Eucharist and a relationship with Mary, the Blessed Virgin Mother. May you increase our devotion to you in the Eucharist. May you bring us closer to your mother and increase our gratitude for your tender love for us expressed through giving us the gift of a mother to care for us as we continue this journey of life.

Amen.

A Place to Reflect

12

THAT NONE
WOULD BE LOST

"Joy!" Matt shouted, no longer seeing his nineteen-month-old daughter in their yard. Then to his wife and kids, he called, "Has anyone seen Joy? Where's Joy?" But no one had seen her. Matt quickly ran across the yard to the fence that enclosed the pool.

To his horror, he saw his beloved Joy face down in the pool. Vaulting the fence, he pulled her out of the water and began CPR, while his wife called 911.

As he tried to save his daughter's life, Matt remembers praying. In between breaths, he begged for the breath of God to bring her life. He offered the words of Jesus, 'Talitha cum,' which means, 'Little girl, I say to you, arise.' He begged for a miracle as he tried to revive his baby daughter.

He continued to pray and perform CPR until the paramedics arrived. They quickly began working on Joy, but it seemed clear to them, based on experience, that they were going to lose her.

As he followed the ambulance to the hospital, Matt pleaded to God the Father for his daughter's life. At one point he prayed, "Father, I know she is your daughter, but she's my daughter too, and now is not the time." The emergency room team did all that they could. Joy's heart was beating, but she needed help breathing and her chances of surviving were slim. Soon, her story went viral on social media, and thousands of people united in praying for Joy's healing.

There is great power in prayer. A week after her arrival at the hospital, Joy could breathe on her own and was taken off the respirator. Not only did she survive, she made a full recovery. Given her condition when she arrived at the hospital, this truly was a miraculous healing.

Later, Matt shared that his heart was deeply torn at Joy's suffering, yet he experienced what could only be called a God-given peace and faith. Through it all, he experienced the strength that comes from knowing who God the Father is and his great love for both him and his daughter.

God's Word

> *"While he was still speaking, a man from the ruler's house came and said, 'Your daughter is dead; do not trouble the Teacher any more.' But Jesus on hearing this answered him, 'Do not fear; only believe, and she shall be well.' ... But taking her by the hand he called, saying, 'Child, arise.' And her spirit returned, and she got up at once" (Luke 8:49–50, 54–55).*

> *"For God so loved the world that he gave his only-begotten Son, that whoever believes in him should not perish but have eternal life" (John 3:16).*

What It Means for Us

This Gospel passage is often referred to as the story of Jairus or the raising of Jairus' daughter. The parallels between this story and that of Matt and his daughter, Joy, are profound. One characteristic of a father's heart—and the Father's heart—is how viscerally he loves his child and wants to save them from loss.

The Gospel tells us that Jairus "fell at Jesus' feet and begged him to come to his house" (Luke 41). Jairus left behind his dignity as a leader of the synagogue, and even in the face of the sure death of his daughter, he cried out to Jesus with hope when there should have been no hope. Why? Because a father continues to hope for his child, fight for his child, and pray for his child when everyone else gives up. No father wants any of his children to be lost.

As Scripture reminds us, "The Lord is not slow about his promise, as some think of slowness, but is patient with you, not wanting any to perish, but all to come to repentance" (2 Peter 3:9). God doesn't want any to perish. He pursues us and fights for us, so that all of us, his children, will receive the gift of eternal life.

So that none would be lost, the Father sent his son, Jesus, as our savior. In our human frailty, we often miss the most important truths because they are so often held before us. Before reading the following verse, reflect on the experience of Matt with his daughter Joy and the experience of Jairus with his daughter. Reflect on the interior experience of a father afraid that they might lose their beloved child. Now read this verse again: "For God so loved the world that he gave his only-begotten Son, that whoever believes in him should not perish but have eternal life" (John 3:16).

It is with this same kind of love that the Father sends his Son. He sent his Son to save us. He continues to pursue us. Why? For our salvation. So that we may have life and have it in abundance. Let us stop fighting him. Let us surrender to his saving work. Let us find life in his saving heart.

Let us pray.

Heavenly Father, we know that we are your children and that you desire none of us to be lost. May the Holy Spirit root us in the truth of who you are and give us the peace and hope necessary to encounter all of life's travails.

Amen.

A Place to Reflect

13

ORDINATION DAY

The big day had finally arrived, a day that I had been pursuing with everything I had for fifteen years. Today, I would be ordained a priest. What a way to be ordained—at St. Patrick's Cathedral in Manhattan by the cardinal archbishop of New York.

There was a slight catch, however. One of my guests was late, and as the clock ticked to twenty minutes and then ten minutes until the start of the ordination Mass, I was beginning to feel some anxiety. This was a special guest, an older priest who was like a spiritual father to me and was flying to New York from California to "vest me" at my ordination. So, I was at the back of the cathedral, dressed in my white alb and holding on to my deacon's stole, waiting for him so I could escort him to his seat. Finally, just a few minutes before we were set to begin the procession, he arrived. I helped him to his seat, returned to the back of the cathedral, and quickly threw on my stole as the organ started to blare.

Thousands of people with huge smiles and phones held up to take videos and pictures watched us as we processed up the steps into the sanctuary of St. Patrick's Cathedral with the huge lights blasting down on us, so bright that I could feel their warmth. I was experiencing the fullness of the joy and excitement of the moment as we lined up in two columns facing the archbishop.

As I looked at the rows of deacons, and soon-to-be priests, in front of me, I saw each man's diaconal stole correctly hung from right to left diagonally across his body. I suddenly realized that my stole was going in the opposite direction; I had put it on backward. There I was, on the day of my ordination, standing under huge spotlights in front of thousands of people with my stole on backward. It would be like a groom having his pants on backward at his wedding.

My first reaction was embarrassment, and I quickly began to feel stressed about what to do. Should I just let it go? Or should I adjust my stole? Finally, when we sat down, I decided to correct matters. As slick as possible (which probably wasn't slick at all), I removed my stole entirely and put it back on correctly.

As I sat there in the aftermath of this embarrassing moment, I was a bit confused. As a deacon, I had been putting my stole on for liturgies for an entire year. But at the big moment, at my ordination, I put it on backward. As I wondered how this happened, I was moved to prayer. And it was one of the most healing moments of prayer I have had in my life.

In my heart, I looked to the Lord, and I said, "Lord, you called me. You called me to be a priest to represent you *in persona Christi*, and I can't even put my clothes on right." At that moment, I felt the Father speak to me: "That's right, I chose you, and I know what I am doing." There was no harshness. I thought the Lord might say, "It's not about you," or "I'm going to do good in spite of you." But no. It was as if he said, "I know you. I'm going to use your gifts and provide for your gaps."

Perhaps this is similar to the interior experience of the psalmist as he writes about how God knew him from the first moment of his being.

God's Word

> "*Three times I begged the Lord about this, that it should leave me; but he said to me, 'My grace is sufficient for you, for my power is made perfect in weakness'*" (2 Corinthians 12:8–9).

*"For you formed my inmost parts, you knitted me together in my
mother's womb. I praise you, for I am wondrously made.
Wonderful are your works! You know me right well; my frame
was not hidden from you, when I was being made in secret,
intricately wrought in the depths of the earth. Your eyes beheld
my unformed substance; in your book were written, every one of
them, the days that were formed for me, when as yet there were
none of them. How precious to me are your thoughts, O God!
How vast the sum of them!" (Psalm 139:13–17).*

What It Means for Us

This experience was so moving to me because, like many of us, I had spent
my life wrestling with perfectionism and a real fear of making mistakes. It
was a burden of anxiety and pressure that I carried. But on the day of my
ordination, the Lord, in prayer, removed from my shoulders the yoke of
perfectionism. He bestowed on me, in the most beautiful way, his yoke—
one that is easy, whose burden is light—the yoke of being his beloved son.

Our Lord Jesus, who reveals the Father to us, offers us this invitation:
"Come to me, all who labor and are heavy laden, and I will give you rest.
Take my yoke upon you, and learn from me; for I am gentle and lowly in
heart" (Matthew 11:28–30). In this invitation, God the Father wants to
free us from the yoke of thinking we have to do it all by ourselves and
be perfect on our own. He wants to bestow upon us the yoke of the sons
and daughters of God, rooted in the truth that we need not be afraid and
anxious about our weakness. It is truly in our places of poverty and need
that his strength is perfected and his glory made manifest.

We can struggle with doubts. We can question if God really knows us.
We can question if he knew what he was doing when he entrusted us with
a task that seems large to us. There can be a part of us that pushes back
and says, "Lord, I think you made a mistake."

But God does not make mistakes. It is a great truth and mystery that God our Father knows us, for he knit us together in our mothers' wombs. He knows all, and he knows us. Knowing all the details, knowing all of our gifts and gaps and strengths and weaknesses and even the mistakes that we will make, he calls us. Whatever our vocation, he entrusts us with this mission, inviting us to trust in his strength. He invites us to trust that his ability to work for the good in all things for those who love him is greater than our ability to mess up his plan for us.

Let us pray.

Heavenly Father, we thank you for the task that you have given us. We thank you for the mission, the invitation to continue to till the soil and to participate in your work in the world. Convince us of the truth that you did not make a mistake in calling us, and root us in the good news and the hope that our inabilities and insecurities are not obstacles to your power, but opportunities for your power to be made perfect. We ask this in Jesus' name.

Amen.

A Place to Reflect

_____

_____

_____

_____

_____

_____

_____

_____

_____

_____

14

ABUNDANCE

As a Franciscan, my call along with my brothers is to love all of the poor and all of our neighbors. But as Jesus had a few special friends—Martha, Mary, and Lazarus, for example—it is natural that some of our neighbors find a special place in the hearts of the friars. One of these neighbors is our dear friend Jamila.

Jamila is a sweet African American woman who has basically experienced every struggle possible in her life. She has suffered from abuse in a variety of ways, and her children suffer with various addictions. She has had health struggles. But she still laughs, and she is still kind. In many ways, she is like a mother to us, especially to the young Franciscan brothers learning our way of life in Harlem. Our ministries are much more relational than simply providing material assistance, so Jamila visits us several times a week.

One day, Jamila knocked at the friary door and asked the brother who answered for some wire cutters. The brother, confused by the request, began to inquire further. Jamila explained that she was asking for the tool because she needed to cut her nails. So, the brother innocently offered, "Well, we do have nail clippers. I could grab those for you." To which Jamila responded, "Thank you brother, but my nails have become so bad that normal clippers aren't strong enough." As the conversation continued,

Jamila shared that in all sixty-plus years of her life, she had never had her nails done. The brother proposed, "If we can make that happen, would you like to have your nails done?" And with her big smile, she said, "Of course. I would love that. I would be delighted." So, the arrangements were made.

One Thursday afternoon, a couple of the young friars took Jamila down to a nearby nail salon and spent the day with her as she got a manicure and pedicure. She received the "queen treatment," which we all agreed she deserved. Jamila just ate up every moment of it, beaming with joy. She received this special gift with a lot of appreciation.

At one point, with a big smile on her face, she looked at the brothers and said, "You know, brothers, I love you so much. You just make me feel like a woman!" The brothers, of course, smiled and laughed, delighted at this little gesture of love. They knew that this outing to the nail salon simply reminded Jamila of the truth of who she is, a beloved daughter and princess of the King of kings.

God's Word

> "I will greatly rejoice in the LORD, my soul shall exult in my God; for he has clothed me with the garments of salvation, he has covered me with the robe of righteousness" (Isaiah 61:10).

> Jesus again said to them ... "I have come that they may have life, and have it abundantly" (John 10:10).

What It Means for Us

When Jesus instituted the sacrament of the Holy Eucharist, giving his Body, Blood, Soul, and Divinity to us under the appearances of bread and wine, there is a profoundly symbolic meaning in how he has chosen to remain with us and to give himself to us.

Bread is simple; it gives sustenance and strength. I think the bread that is changed into the Body of Christ represents God giving us salvation. He gives us the truth and guides us. He gives us what we need to survive so we can make it to heaven. Bread is a staple, and that nourishment is necessary for us to live.

But wine, though? Is wine strictly necessary for life? We could say that it is water—not wine—that is equivalent to bread, as water is all we need for life. Yet Our Lord gives himself to us under the appearance of wine, which has a sweetness to it. Wine shows us that his Presence is not just enough, it is *more than* enough.

Jesus said that he came not just to give us life but to give us life in abundance (see John 10:10). God desires for us not just to survive but to have joy. So he gives us the gift of himself under the appearance of wine. We can see this when Our Lord changed the water into wine at the wedding feast at Cana. Our heavenly Father desires our lives to be filled with joy, song, and light. One might even say he desires to "spoil" us, as the brothers wanted to treat Jamila by helping her get her nails done.

Rooted in this truth, may we have the confidence to share our whole hearts with Jesus—all of our desires, both little and big. May we bring to him with confidence not just what we need to "get by" but also what we want and what we delight in. In the midst of life's crosses, let us trust that God will always give us what is best for us. Let us recognize the truth that God the Father delights in our delight—and that he desires to nourish us. He gives us the Body and Blood of his Son, under the appearance of bread and wine—what we need, but also strength and joy for the journey.

Let us pray.

Heavenly Father, we know that you delight in our delight and that you have come to give us life in abundance. You reveal these things that we might have joy and that our joy might be complete. Through the gift of your Holy Spirit, may we experience this life not just as a valley of

*tears to endure but also as a land flowing with milk and honey and joy
because of our relationship with you. We ask this in Jesus' name.*

Amen.

A Place to Reflect

_____

_____

_____

_____

_____

_____

_____

_____

_____

_____

_____

_____

_____

_____

_____

_____

_____

_____

_____

_____

_____

_____

_____

_____

_____

_____

15

A SHIELD

There are stories of certain friars that we love to tell. Sometimes, we hesitate telling these stories because we don't want people to think they reflect the lives of every Franciscan. There is one brother in particular, Brother Kolbe, who has a beautiful and moving willingness to enter into the challenges of life. His goodness is humbling because many of us struggle to imitate it.

One of our favorite stories about Brother Kolbe is the time he and another friar were winding their way through New York traffic along side streets on the way to visit a neighbor in the hospital. They were stopped at a light in Harlem, and Brother Kolbe looked out the window and saw a man and woman ferociously berating a young teenage boy. They were in his face, aggressively shouting at him, "You're a bully! You're a bully!" Brother Kolbe turned to the brother who was driving and said, "We have to do something." His heart was already invested, so he jumped out of the car and fell on his knees between the adults and the teen. From his knees, and with his hands raised, Brother Kolbe started to shout, "Stop! Stop! I was a bully, too. I was a bully, too!"

The couple were immediately paralyzed by the surprising action of this medieval-looking monk who had just entered into the situation. The woman was quickly brought to her senses. The man, while no longer shouting, still showed anger and aggression on his face. As the yelling stopped and everyone's eyes were on Brother Kolbe, he said, "Thank you for stopping. Now, let's pray an Our Father together." The man contemptuously said, "We don't have time for that God stuff right now." But the woman chastised him, saying, "You can't say no to God. You always have to make time for him." So all of them, including the teenage boy they were berating, prayed the Our Father together and then peacefully went their separate ways.

God's Word

"But a Samaritan, as he journeyed, came to where he was; and when
he saw him, he had compassion, and went to him and bound up
his wounds, pouring on oil and wine; then he sat him on his own
beast and brought him to an inn, and took care of him."
(Luke 10:33–34).

"The scribes and the Pharisees brought a woman who had been caught
in adultery ... Jesus bent down and wrote with his finger on the
ground. And as they continued to ask him, he stood up and said
to them, 'Let him who is without sin among you be the first to
throw a stone at her' ... But when they heard it, they went away,
one by one, beginning with the eldest" (John 8:3, 6–7, 9).

What It Means for Us

In the parable of the Good Samaritan, the movement of the man passing by on the side of the road begins in his heart. As the Gospel tells us, he was "moved with pity." Although the Samaritan had never met the suffering man, his heart was given to him. He understood, "This is my brother. This could have been me." So he interrupted his journey and freely attended to the suffering of his brother. It wasn't the convenient choice, nor was it the safe choice, but it was the right choice. It is what Jesus does for us always.

We can see this in the incident when the Pharisees brought Jesus the woman who had been caught in adultery. Surrounded by those who wished to stone her for her transgression, Jesus was asked his opinion about what they should do. He did not do the comfortable thing or the safe thing; he did the right thing. Brother Kolbe did not stay in the car, pretending that he did not see what was happening. He placed himself in the middle of a chaotic situation, he did the right thing—he entered into it and brought about a peaceful resolution.

Jesus, with his bold answer, probably shocked everyone present, making them uncomfortable by going against the grain in a bold way. With his presence and his words, he shielded the woman and protected her. He took upon himself the punishment that the crowd desired to inflict on her. Although they did not stone her that day, Jesus would be beaten and condemned on Good Friday in atonement for her sin and the sins of all the world. He protected her, taking her punishment upon himself.

As our Savior, Jesus gives us this beautiful insight into the Father's heart. He is not indifferent to what is going on in our lives—and he does not hesitate to get involved. He is always ready to do something bold. He does not count the cost, because his heart is given over to the good of his children. Jesus takes upon himself our transgressions and shields us. And for this, may he always be praised.

Let us pray.

Heavenly Father, we praise you and thank you for having your Son take upon himself our transgressions and the punishment for our sins, even though he never committed sin. We thank you for the ways throughout history you have provided for your people. You are a shade and shield for us. We thank you for the ways you protect us, guard our dignity, and cover us from shame. We thank you, Father, for being deeply invested in every moment of our lives, especially those moments where we feel most isolated and most ashamed. May we repent of our sins and continue to find rest and refuge in you. We ask this in Jesus' name.

Amen.

A Place to Reflect

16

"ALL THAT IS
MINE IS YOURS"

As I looked out the second-floor window of the shelter and saw the all-black SUVs with tinted windows parked out front, I knew what it meant: the police commissioner was back to help cook and serve dinner.

For many years, a collection of active or retired New York Police Department (NYPD) officers of different faiths and backgrounds have come once a week to help prepare dinner at our homeless shelter. In time, the police commissioner heard about it and started to come when he could.

The NYPD commissioner is appointed by the mayor of New York to head the largest police department in the United States, with nearly 36,000 officers. Due to the nature of his position and the danger it entails, the commissioner does not just show up at a location; an advance team arrives first and searches the area to ensure it is secure. Though he couldn't come to the shelter every week, he came often enough that he got to know some of its residents, all of whom were men except for Amy. Because she was the shelter's only woman, the commissioner soon learned her story.

Amy was in her early sixties and was dying of cancer. She was a long-term guest in a private area of the shelter due to her terminal illness. For about six months, the friars had made an accommodation for her in a guest room so they could look after her and help her get to doctor's appointments. She became somewhat of the "mom" at the shelter. She offered both encouragement and correction when the time was right to our missionary volunteers and to the men, keeping everybody in check and well-behaved.

When the commissioner heard Amy's story, he was moved and got to know her. He would grab a seat and spend extra time with her as the meal was being served or before he left for the evening.

As with any terminal illness, Amy's condition continued to worsen. Eventually, after receiving the last sacraments, she passed away. When the commissioner learned of her death, he immediately called Fr. Ignatius, the director of the homeless shelter, and said that he wanted to give Amy a formal NYPD funeral. So, in the small church next door, with the friars, homeless men, and several volunteers, we celebrated Amy's funeral Mass. Outside, rows of NYPD motorcycles, patrol cars, color guard, and bagpipers waited to escort her body to its final resting place.

To this day, we often speak of Amy's funeral and how the police commissioner, with all of his authority and prestige, treated her in such a special way. His desire to give her such recognition echoed the words shared between Jesus and his Father: "All mine are yours."

God's Word

> *"He lifted up his eyes to heaven and said, 'Father, the hour has come; glorify your Son that the Son may glorify you ... all mine are yours, and yours are mine'" (John 17:1, 10).*

What It Means for Us

These words of Jesus are found in his high priestly prayer, as he speaks with his Father. They are the same words that we hear the good father speak to the elder son in the parable of the prodigal son: "All that is mine is yours" (Luke 15:31). Isn't this the truth about our heavenly Father? A good earthly father says to his children, to those he loves, "All I have is yours. All my resources are yours. Whatever you need, whatever you ask for, whatever I can do, I'm going to do."

I think the story of the police commissioner is deeply moving because of how he—a man of worldly honor and responsibility in many ways—found in his heart a special place for this poor, lonely, sick woman. He lavished upon Amy all of his resources to celebrate her life by allowing her to be buried with a particular dignity and reverence.

How much more does our heavenly Father look upon each of us in our lowliness and say, "All I have is yours. Ask and you will receive. Seek and you will find. Knock and the door will be opened to you" (see Matthew 7:7).

Now, of course, this does not mean that every prayer will be answered according to the timeline and mode that we see as best, but our heavenly Father has no desire to hold anything back. The gift that he desires to give, above all, is the gift of his very self, which he communicates to us first and foremost through the sacraments, but also as we call upon him and invite him into our hearts, our poverty, and our pain.

Before his return to the Father, Jesus told his disciples, "And see, I am sending upon you what my Father promised; so stay here in the city until you have been clothed with power from on high" (Luke 24:49). What, or better yet *who*, is the promise of the Father? The Holy Spirit.

This is the response that God gives us throughout salvation history. This is the gift he gives to us in our poverty and need. He gives the gift of his very self, the greatest gift possible. In our suffering, insecurity, uncertainty, and struggles, he gives us his very life. In giving us himself, he gives to us all that he is and has. The gift of himself is the gift of everything.

Let us turn to him with radical confidence, to be filled anew with the grace, faith, hope, and charity, the confidence and strength that are ours as we receive more and more of God's very life within us.

Let us pray.

Heavenly Father, I believe that you are the most generous of fathers and you desire to hold nothing back from your beloved child. Help me to believe you when you say that all that is yours is mine. I ask again to be filled and made new with the gift of the Holy Spirit so that your life alive in me may guide me and strengthen me again this day. We ask this in Jesus' name.

Amen.

A Place to Reflect

17

THE FREEDOM OF THE FATHER'S CHILD

Due to some personal struggles and challenges, Jamie's parents were not able to take care of her.

So, for most of her life, eleven-year-old Jamie had been in and out of foster care.

Those who serve in the social services system certainly try their best to take care of the children in their care, but this is a difficult task. Like many kids in the foster care system, Jamie moved between several foster homes, staying in one for a while and hoping it might be her "forever" home, then being forced to move again. As one foster home after another reached its capacity and was unable to care for her any longer, she began to develop a sense that she was a burden on others. Eventually, she was sent to the home of the Pickett's, who decided to adopt her. This would be her home forever.

One Saturday afternoon, Mr. Pickett, Jamie's new dad, was in his office doing some of the household finances when she walked in. Jamie handed him a handful of dollar bills and coins totaling $7.45 and said, "Here, Dad. This is for you."

Her dad put down his pen, took off his reading glasses, and looked at her. With some confusion, he asked, "What is this for?" She said, "Well, I've been saving money, and I want to give it to you to help contribute to the family. I know it is expensive to have me here. So here is what I have to help with the cost of things around the house."

As he heard these words, Mr. Pickett's heart was wrenched, and he reached out to Jamie and held her hands. He looked her in the eyes and said, "Jamie, this is your home. I'm your dad, and you're my daughter. I want you to be an eleven-year-old, to laugh, play, and have fun. I want you to be a little girl who knows that she's home and knows that she's wanted and loved. So, put that money back in your pocket. You never need to think that you need to pay or do anything to earn your place here. This is your home."

So often, brothers and sisters, in our relationship with God, we place a burden on ourselves like Jamie placed on herself in her new home. We can think we have to earn love. But God the Father calls us to freedom. As we see, St. Paul writes about this in his letter to the Galatians.

God's Word

> *"For freedom Christ has set us free; stand fast therefore, and do not submit again to a yoke of slavery ... For you were called to freedom, brethren; only do not use your freedom as an opportunity for the flesh, but through love be servants of one another"* (Galatians 5:1, 13).

What It Means for Us

Jamie thought she had to earn her father's love and her place in his home. This mistaken attitude can creep into our lives in our relationship with God. We can try to be perfect and perform well in order to earn his love, prove that we are good, and have a place in the Kingdom. There can be a tendency to equate our worth with what we can *do* rather than who we *are* in God's eyes. But we are invited to the freedom of the sons of God.

One of the great masters on the concept of freedom is Fr. Jacques Philippe, particularly in his book *Interior Freedom*. He writes, "Human beings are more than the sum of the good they can accomplish. They are children of God, whether they do good or cannot yet manage to do anything. Our Father in heaven does not love us because of the good we do, he loves us for ourselves because he has adopted us as his children forever."[2]

We love others, worship God, and follow the commandments; we do good, pray, fast, and give alms. These are all good things, but they need to be rightly ordered. We do these things, first and foremost, as a response of gratitude and of love for God and love for others for his sake. We do these things as an outpouring of the generous gift that we have received from God, his love for us. In his love, he has made us his adopted sons and daughters—and others our brothers and sisters—in Christ.

We are troubled and burdened when we try to do spiritual things to prove something or to earn God's love or acceptance. Like Jamie, it is as if we are saying, "Here's what I am bringing to the table so that I have a home here." This attitude comes from insecurity, as if our home is in jeopardy and that the rug can be pulled out from under us anytime. The hard news is we couldn't afford the rent anyway. The good news is that his love is freely given. The freedom of the sons of God is to know that we have an eternal home with him. We don't have to earn his love. But we do have to receive it, remain in it, and respond to it with gratitude and generosity.

To quote from Fr. Phillipe again, "[God] loves us for ourselves, because he has adopted us as his children forever." Let us always remember that we are his children—and that we have a home in him that remains forever.

---

2. Jacques Philippe, *Interior Freedom*, trans. Helena Scott (New York: Scepter, 2007), 124.

Let us pray.

Heavenly Father, how deeply I desire a home. Yet how deeply I feel like a stranger and sojourner in this land as if I need to prove, to accomplish, to earn my place, and to protect my place. In you, help me find authentic rest, authentic freedom, as your child. Help me to know that in you I have an eternal home because you love me for myself. In response to this security, may I pour myself out in love of you and love of my brothers and sisters with great generosity. I ask this in Jesus' name.

Amen.

A Place to Reflect

_____

_____

_____

_____

_____

_____

_____

_____

_____

_____

_____

_____

_____

_____

_____

_____

_____

_____

18

FIGHTING FOR YOU

When Lily was eight years old, her mother sat her down and said, "Never expect anything from a man. Men will always let you down and disappoint you." The unfortunate truth is that Lily not only heard these words at such a young age, but they were confirmed by her experience with her father, who struggled with addiction.

One day that Lily never forgot, she went with friends to a park about a fifteen-minute drive from her house. At the end of the outing, she realized she didn't have a ride home. So, naturally, she called her dad and asked him to pick her up.

Lily's dad came. He didn't say a word the entire drive back home, but as they pulled into the driveway, he looked at her and said, "Never ask me to do something like that for you ever again." Of course, Lily's young heart shriveled, and tears welled up in her eyes as her father got out and walked into the house, frustrated by the inconvenience of being a father. In the years that followed, there were times Lily would walk two hours to get someplace rather than call her dad and ask for even a few minutes of his time.

This experience of masculinity and fatherhood hurt her deeply. Growing up in the Catholic Faith, Lily felt unable to pray to Jesus or to God the Father because she believed there was nothing that a man could offer. As she got older, these struggles would manifest themselves in rebellion and acting out.

One of our friaries had a youth group near where Lily lived, and she occasionally attended with some of her friends. But she was often difficult and combative, especially toward the friars. The brothers got to know her, and Brother Francis always tried to look out for her. When he saw her breaking the rules, he would confront her and also call her mother. He did everything he could, but things got to the point where Lily was not willing to listen at all.

For eight years, Brother Francis tried to look out for Lily and to win her trust, but she fought him every step of the way and did everything she could to push him away. Her behavior during youth group would sometimes be so disruptive that it would ruin the experience for everyone. In her woundedness, anger, and fear of being hurt, Lily gave Brother Francis every reason to give up on her, but he did not. As a good spiritual father, he fought for her.

When the opportunity came up to go with the youth group on a pilgrimage, Lily went with them. There was a heatwave when they arrived, and many in the group fell ill in the heat. As always, Brother Francis looked out for Lily, who was not taking care of herself, making sure that she ate, but Lily, as usual, still reacted to him argumentatively. Then one morning, Brother Francis needed to go and help another youth group member who was sick. Before he left, he gave Lily a sandwich he had packed for her. He said, "Right now, I need to help someone else, so here is your lunch. You know what to do. You got this."

At that moment, something about Brother Francis' act released something in Lily. She saw that, for eight years, he had shown concern for her and fought for her, even though she resisted him every step of the way. She realized that he kept her in mind even as he was caring for someone else.

Though Lily's wounds from her upbringing did not immediately disappear, slowly but surely she began to experience real healing in her heart and in her ability to give and receive in her relationships. Brother Francis continued to walk with Lily, but in a new way as she grew to trust him. Over time, Lily's life became radically transformed, and she welcomed Jesus into her life.

A few years after her conversion to deeper faith, Lily developed a relationship with a young man, who eventually asked her to marry him. Since her father had passed away, Lily asked Brother Francis to walk her down the aisle. The wedding was celebrated in Canada during the COVID-19 lockdown, so Brother Francis had to arrive two weeks before the ceremony to quarantine. He willingly made this sacrifice to celebrate this joyous occasion with Lily. How beautiful it was that the Lord provided Lily with a spiritual father who would freely give two weeks of his life to her—she who had learned as a child never to ask her father even for fifteen minutes.

God's Word

> "When the season of fruit drew near, he sent his servants to the tenants, to get his fruit; and the tenants took his servants and beat one, killed another, and stoned a third. Again he sent other servants, more than the first; and they did the same to them. Afterward he sent his son to them, saying, 'They will respect my son'" (Matthew 21:34–37).

> "Then Pilate took Jesus and scourged him. And the soldiers plaited a crown of thorns, and put it on his head, and clothed him in a purple robe; they came up to him, saying, 'Hail, King of the Jews!' and struck him with their hands" (John 19:1–3).

What It Means for Us

In the Gospel, Jesus talks about how his Father had sent prophet after prophet to call his people to repentance. In the end, he sent his own Son, who they rejected and had crucified.

Throughout salvation history, God the Father has never given up on us. Today, he continues to fight for you and me. Jesus came to earth and spent his whole life fighting for us, even to the point of shedding his blood for our salvation. Through our rebellion, rejection, and indifference, he fights to win us over. He never stops fighting to heal our lack of trust and claim us as his own.

Like Brother Francis fought for Lily, God the Father fights for each of us. May his fight for each of us bring us healing. May his refusal to give up on us heal our wounds and help us to trust him. May his pursuit of us be medicine for our interior rebellion and self-protection and reveal the truth that we are wanted.

The truth is that God loves you, and he is willing to fight for you. Every day of your life, he has fought for you, and he continues to fight for your time, for your heart, and for your trust. May each of us allow ourselves to be conquered by his love.

Let us pray.

Heavenly Father, thank you for fighting for us. We repent of the ways in which we push you away and place barriers against your loving pursuit of us. Heal our wounds. Heal our inclination to "protect" ourselves from you. Heal our doubts. May your grace allow us to surrender to your pursuit, so we might allow your love more fully into our lives. We ask this in Jesus' name.

Amen.

A Place to Reflect

19

HIS STRONG ARMS

After being blessed with six biological children, the O'Reilly's were open to adoption if God called them to do so. One day, they learned of twins, Connor and Lisa, who needed a home. They were eight years old.

Due to some difficult circumstances in the lives of their parents, including substance abuse, Connor and Lisa had been born with mental disabilities and had been in and out of the foster care system.

These young children needed a generous and caring home because they were not going to be easy to care for. They would always be dependent on their parents. The O'Reilly's hearts were moved, and after some discernment and discussion with their family, they decided to open their home to Connor and Lisa. Caring for them stretched their capacities as parents, but they loved them with their whole hearts.

Because of their life experience, at times, Connor and Lisa would respond to some stimuli or fear by yelling. They would scream and shake and hit whatever was around them, even to the detriment of their own safety.

When Connor or Lisa would start to go into one of these reactive episodes, Mr. O'Reilly always responded in the same way. He would go to the child who was screaming and shouting, and kicking and punching, and he would wrap his strong arms around them, hold them tight, keeping their arms down, and hugging them. He wouldn't tell them to be quiet or shout at them. In fact, he would never say a word. He would just hold them as they screamed and shook until they calmed down. Then, he would simply say, "I love you," kiss them on the forehead, and let them go about their day.

In this story, we see a truth about our heavenly Father. He is all-powerful. In his strength, he can handle whatever anger or questions or frustrations we bring him.

God's Word

"How long, O LORD? Will you forget me forever?
How long will you hide your face from me?
How long must I bear pain in my soul,
and have sorrow in my heart all the day?" (Psalm 13:1–2)

What It Means for Us

The psalms of lament are particularly moving. Perhaps the most famous of these is Psalm 22, some of the words of which are on Jesus' lips as he hangs on the Cross: "My God, My God, why have you forsaken me?" (Psalm 22:1). In the lament psalms, the psalmist is crying out to God, "Why? Why is this hard thing happening to me and my people? Where are you? Have you abandoned me?"

Our Father is all-powerful, and he can handle such difficult and agonized questions. Since the primary author of the book of Psalms (as with all of Scripture) is God himself, he has not only given us permission to express our frustrations, sorrows, and our difficulties but shows us how to do this. He models how we should be totally vulnerable, raw, and real with him. The Father wants us to come as we are, expressing what we really feel, in our relationship with him.

Jesus gives us a beautiful example in his agony in the garden of Gethsemane when he prays, "Father, if you are willing, remove this chalice from me" (Luke 22:42). In the garden, he brings his profound suffering to his Father. He remains committed to his Father's will and shows us how to be open to his ability to bring good out of anything. It might seem as if the Father is silent during Jesus' crucifixion and three days in the tomb, but he is holding him—and the entire world—in his strong but tender arms until the Resurrection.

Mr. O'Reilly was not afraid to hold his children during their tantrums and shouting. He gave them a safe place for their struggles—his loving arms, in relationship with him.

All of us experience difficulties and struggles in life, even tragedies. The Lord is not asking us to hide our struggles from him or pretend that they do not exist. Rather, he is inviting us to be in relationship with him as we experience all our sorrows, doubts, and questions. He is inviting us to trust in his strength and his goodness.

Connor and Lisa's outbursts are harmful when they have them on their own. When they are left to their own devices, apart from their father, that's when they can really hurt themselves and hurt others. Similarly, we're not meant to suffer and lament apart from our Father, but in relationship with him. When we try and deal with it apart from him is when we hurt others and ourselves, but if we bring it to him, in his arms we find a place to take our doubts and pain, but also safety and peace.

May we find rest in his strength and protection, knowing that he is with us in our difficulties. In our struggles, he wants us to come all the closer to him. May we have confidence that all aspects of our lives are under the care and the embrace of our heavenly Father, until the day when Christ comes again in glory and all will be revealed.

Let us pray.

Heavenly Father, my pains and sorrows, difficulties and questions become all the more painful and heavy as I try to carry them on my own. I bring these to you now, Lord. Through the grace of the Holy Spirit, grant me the guidance, freedom, and wisdom to be real with you and help me to stay in relationship with you. Give me the confidence to entrust all of my heart and all of my needs to your loving arms, trusting that you are at work in my life and that your presence is my peace.

Amen.

A Place to Reflect

_____
_____
_____
_____
_____
_____
_____
_____
_____
_____
_____
_____
_____
_____
_____
_____
_____
_____
_____
_____
_____
_____
_____
_____

20

HE NEVER TIRES

As we grow older, we can often look back on our lives, particularly childhood, and reflect on the past in light of our later experiences.

Thinking back on my own life, particularly in preparation for this book, I reflected that my father never stopped an activity we were doing together and said, "OK, that's enough." As an uncle playing with my nieces or as a priest visiting families and spending time with their children, I have, at times, said, "OK, let's take a break." But I never remember hearing those words from my dad.

I remember throwing the football with my dad. We would play catch with a Nerf football in the house. He had a spot in the corner on the couch, and I would run a little five-yard post route around a support beam. He would throw the ball, and I would cut and run and catch it. I remember running that route again and again and again. As long as I was willing to keep running and catching the ball, he would keep throwing it. This was true in all sports, and it was true in schoolwork as well. He never said, "OK, let's stop" or, "I need a break."

I realize now that he was able to match my youthful energy because of his love. When it came to me, his son—playing or just spending time with me—my dad was always ready for more.

This is true of our heavenly Father, as well, in the area of forgiveness. As Pope Francis reminds us, "The God of mercy ... does not tire of forgiving. We are the ones who tire in asking for forgiveness, but he does not tire."[3]

God's Word

> "The steadfast love of the LORD never ceases,
>> his mercies never come to an end;
>> they are new every morning;
>> great is your faithfulness" (Lamentations 3:22–23).

What It Means for Us

In my own life as a sinner and penitent, I get frustrated with myself. While I have a regular habit of going to confession, at times I don't want to have to go and again confessing the same sin. I am tired of it. I am embarrassed by it. But what Pope Francis reminds us, and what my dad taught me from a young age, is that the Father never tires of us. He never tires of bringing us back to life. He never tires of receiving us. He never tires of forgiving us.

Scripture tells us that God's mercies are new every morning. Every day, he is willing to forgive us again. Again and again, he renews his mercy for us. Jesus told us, "Be merciful, even as your Father is merciful" (Luke 6:36), and when Peter asked him how often he had to forgive others, Jesus said, "I do not say to you seven times, but seventy times seven" (Matthew 18:22). In other words, we must never stop forgiving because God our Father never stops. The mercy of the heavenly Father is an untiring mercy.

As I have shared, sometimes I need to ask for a break. I cannot match my father's ability to keep going. I find a similar struggle with extending mercy. At times I want to say, "I've forgiven enough! I need a break." To

---

3. Quoted in "God Never Tires of Forgiving Us, Pope Reflects," Catholic News Agency, March 28, 2014, catholicnewsagency.com.

this we are called to remember our Father's mercy toward us and to "be perfect as our Father in heaven is perfect" (Matthew 5:48).

When it comes to us and our needs, when we turn to him for his time and attention, when we need his healing and mercy, our Father in heaven never says, "OK, that's enough." He is always there, ready to receive us and to restore us again and again.

My brothers and sisters, let us give thanks to the Lord, for he is good; for his mercy endures forever.

Let us pray.

Heavenly Father, give me confidence in your untiring mercy, in your untiring love of me. As I get tired of returning to forgiveness, may your goodness, your love, and your spirit alive within me strengthen me. Give me the grace never to cease returning to you. I ask this in Jesus' name.

Amen.

A Place to Reflect

Part 3
The Father's Call to Us

21

TAKING THE TIME

Molly had made it all the way to problem number 21 of her thirty-part algebra homework before she hit a snag. It was one she had encountered before. The truth was that she didn't fully understand the math required for the assignment, but she had been able to fake it up to this point. Though she was able to "fake it" for some of the other questions, she couldn't figure out problem 21. So, Molly faced a dilemma: she could either not do this assignment and get lectured by Ms. Chang at school or she could ask for her father's help, but at a cost.

After deliberating for a few minutes, she decided to try her luck with her dad. So, she went and asked him, "Hey, Dad, can you help me with one of my algebra problems?" She pulled up a chair next to him at the table, and he said, "OK, show me what you did." Molly showed him what she had tried to do, but then what she was afraid would happen did. Her father went back to the start of the chapter to teach her the entire unit from the beginning! So, a thirty-minute lesson began, with her dad actually helping her understand the math that she needed to learn to do problem 21.

As her father went through his lesson, Molly became impatient and frustrated, wishing she could just get up and leave. But her dad had realized that, since she didn't really understand her math homework, he needed to help her learn it. That happened every time Molly asked her father for help because he cared about her learning, even more than she did. So, whenever she brought a problem to him, he would not just give her a quick answer. He would sit her down and help her really learn the lesson. This became a bit of a joke in the family, but these were lessons that would end up serving Molly very well later in life.

Many of us have experienced something like this with our own fathers, teachers, or coaches. As we see in Scripture, this was the story of the people of Israel throughout salvation history.

God's Word

God told the Israelites, "But as for you, turn, and journey into the wilderness in the direction of the Red Sea" (Deuteronomy 1:40).

"For my thoughts are not your thoughts, neither are your ways my ways, says the LORD.
For as the heavens are higher than the earth, so are my ways higher than your ways and my thoughts than your thoughts" (Isaiah 55:8–9).

What It Means for Us

Like Molly with her dad, we often go to a teacher or mentor wanting a quick answer because we just want them to solve our immediate problem so we can move on. A good leader, though, will make us pause and do the hard work because they want us actually to *learn*, to grow in our understanding. Ultimately, although it can be frustrating in the moment, their approach is for our greater good.

We cannot help but think of the people of Israel fleeing from slavery in Egypt to the Promised Land of Canaan, the land flowing with milk and honey. Scripture tells us that God did not take them on the quickest path. Instead, he had them journey for forty years in the desert, leading them with fire by night and cloud by day, feeding them with manna and quail.

Why didn't God lead them directly to the Promised Land? Because he cared about their formation. He cared about whether they learned about his presence and his providential love for them. He cared about whether they were purified from the bad habits, sinful ways, and false idols they picked up in Egypt. The LORD cared for them even more than they cared for themselves. Even though they complained and murmured in the desert, God kept teaching them and forming them because it was what was best for them in the end.

Like the Israelites, we can be tempted to become impatient with God's ways and his timeline. God's ways just are not our ways, and his timeline is not our timeline. This can be a point of frustration and difficulty that can tempt us to cry out and murmur, "Where are you, God? What are you doing?" Sometimes it can even cause us to hesitate to follow him because we are afraid of what he is doing in our lives.

But God is good; he is our loving Father. He says, "My thoughts are not your thoughts, neither are your ways my ways" (Isaiah 55:8). But he also tells us, "No eye has seen, nor ear heard, nor the heart of man conceived, what God has prepared for those who love him" (1 Corinthians 2:9).

The heavenly Father is always at work in our lives, and he is always teaching us. He acts in his own time, not because he delights in frustrating us but because he is zealous for our good, our sanctification, and our purification. He desires that our joy may be complete. May confidence in God's fatherhood and his goodness help us to be patient and trust him during times of trial. May we trust his care for us on this pilgrimage of life in which he continues to lead us each day. Ultimately, he is leading us toward the eternal Promised Land, to unity with him forever.

Let us pray.

Heavenly Father, help me to trust in your goodness. May trusting who you are help me to trust the path you have me on and the timeline by

which you continue to work your plan for my life. Help me to trust
your ways and your timeline more than my own because you desire
my good with the fullness of a father's love. I ask this in Jesus' name.

Amen.

A Place to Reflect

_____
_____
_____
_____
_____
_____
_____
_____
_____
_____
_____
_____
_____
_____
_____
_____
_____
_____
_____
_____
_____
_____
_____
_____
_____
_____

22

LOST IN THE DESERT

For the last several years, Fr. Innocent, the postulant director of the Franciscan Friars of the Renewal, has taken our postulants on a yearly wilderness hiking trip. Along with COR missionaries affiliated with a Catholic college in Wyoming, they go on a three-week backpacking excursion in the Moab desert. The trip includes rock climbing, canyoneering, and rappelling. For twenty-one tough days, the men carry heavy packs, battle the elements, endure cold nights, and go without basic amenities such as showers. It is an opportunity for them to experience their capacity as men in a new way. More importantly, though, it is a time for them to experience the great Christian tradition of desert spirituality, in which God the Father speaks to his people in the poverty of the Wilderness in a most beautiful and intimate way.

One of the challenges of these desert trips is that the postulants, in pairs, take turns acting as "leaders of the day" (or LODs). When each man's turn comes, it is his responsibility to work with his partner and lead the rest of the group from the starting point to that day's campsite. The LODs are responsible for navigating the land.

On one backpacking trip, there were fourteen of us, and we were carrying our rations for the week. Together with our pots and pans and tents and water, that meant that we were all carrying packs weighing between sixty-five to seventy pounds.

On one particular day, we were on a cliff face, looking down into a canyon. The LODs got to one point in the terrain, which, according to the map, was the place to drop down into canyon. Once we got to the bottom, we could begin walking for the four or five hours it would take to get to our campsite for that evening. The LODs looked down the path out of the canyon and judged it to be a little too difficult. They assumed that if they kept walking around the canyon, they would find an easier path. They deliberated for a moment, then communicated their decision to the rest of the team, and we began walking. We walked past that exit and began following the LODs on into the canyon.

The wilderness guides, who accompany the group and are responsible for keeping us safe, dropped back to speak to the priests who were on the trip with the postulants. The guides said, "Hey, just so you know, that was the only drop in, so we're going to have to walk all around this canyon until we get back here. It's about to be a really long day." This is exactly what happened.

The entire team, each carrying his heavy pack, walked for hours to get back to that initial exit. What was intended to be a five- or six-hour trek turned out to be a ten-hour day, with a few hurt ankles along the way as guys got a little less surefooted toward the end. While they tried to push on, eventually the leaders made the call that we were not going to make it to the campsite and that we were going to have to sleep in the canyon. Ultimately, we made up the lost time the next day and everything was all right, but it was a really challenging day.

The guides' decision to allow the LODs to learn from their mistake can help us meditate on a truth about God the Father.

God's Word

> *"Since then we have a great high priest who has passed through the
> heavens, Jesus, the Son of God, let us hold fast our confession. For
> we have not a high priest who is unable to sympathize with our
> weaknesses, but one who in every respect has been tempted as we
> are, yet without sinning. Let us then with confidence draw near
> to the throne of grace, that we may receive mercy and find grace
> to help in time of need"* (Hebrews 4:14–16).

> *"We know that in everything God works for good with those who love
> him, who are called according to his purpose"* (Romans 8:28).

What It Means for Us

I think this story of the postulants' hiking trip can communicate two important truths. The guides and priests knew the decision being made was wrong and that it was going to be a long day. They could have just said, "No, this is the only path," and that would have saved the entire group an extra six or seven hours of hiking with seventy-pound packs. But they didn't because they were there at the service of the men, allowing them to learn and grow. They were going to be with the postulants in the journey, struggling and suffering with them, while looking out for them to ensure there were no serious consequences to their mistake.

As good fathers and teachers, the priests did not choose the easy route. These postulants were not in the desert just to get from point A to point B. Instead, they were there to learn and grow as men. Often, the Lord does this with us, as well, allowing us the time to take the long route. But he is always there with us. He is Emmanuel, God with us, present with us in the struggle.

There is also an opportunity in this story to look at the distinction between how God directly wills something and how he simply allows something—even something that seems bad—for a greater good. On that trip, what if the LODs had asked the priests and guides, "Hey, is there an easier exit?" And what if the guides had said, "Sure, keep walking, and we will take the easier path." Then, an hour later, they said, "No, we were just kidding. We wanted you to have to walk all those extra hours." Obviously, that would have been a great breach of trust. It would have been a deception and a direct choice to cause pain for no reason.

However, what actually happened was different. The guides and priests respected that the LODs were the leaders for the day and that they were in charge of making this decision. The LODs did not ask for guidance, and the guides and priests allowed them the freedom to make their own decision—even though they knew it was the wrong decision and that it was going to have a cost. This was not deception or injustice. And it was allowed because they knew a greater good would come, and a great lesson would be learned, through the mistake.

We may struggle with the difficult question of how God, who is all-good, all-knowing, and all-powerful, can allow suffering without directly causing or willing it to happen. God does not will bad things but he does permit them. I think this story of the desert can help us understand that God is a good and loving Father even when he allows difficult things to occur.

The Lord has given us freedom. But we exercise this freedom in a fallen world. Unfortunately, as a result of this freedom, we can sin and make mistakes that can cause great pain. But God remains with us in all things; he is always at work redeeming us and bringing new life out of our brokenness and struggles.

Through the Incarnation, God the Father sent his Son to enter into our struggles, becoming a man like us in all things except sin. We trust that he sees us, loves us, and is always with us. God is at work in all things for the good of those who love him (see Romans 8:28).

Let us pray.

Heavenly Father, at times, your ways confuse me and frustrate me. Give me the grace to trust that you are with me on the journey, that you are at work for the good, and that you have an eternal plan for my life. Help me not to rebel but to trust that you have a divine capacity and creativity to bring good out of evil in my life. I ask this in Jesus' name.

Amen.

A Place to Reflect

23

DYING TO SELF

Novitiate is like a spiritual boot camp, and its leader is like a spiritual drill instructor. The novitiate is a stage of formation that lasts for at least a year following postulancy, at the very beginning of one's entry into religious life. At the end of this period, a man or woman is ready to profess vows within a religious community. The novitiate is dedicated to interior growth, and one of the fruits of this discipline is that a novice has to face himself for who he truly is.

In my own novitiate, our novice master took his job very seriously and set a high standard. In our work of formation these days, particularly in the United States, we find the need to help our young men learn how to die to themselves, to help them not to run and hide when they encounter their own weakness or some sort of conflict or difficulty.

During novitiate, I can recall some moments when I was really being tried and tested. I grew up as a "country club" kid, so there is a part of me that likes comfort more than I should. One day, during the first week, the other novices and I were cleaning and moving things in the garage. As we worked, I realized we were going to need at least twenty minutes to put everything back where it needed to be.

In our community at the time, there was what we called the four o'clock hour. At four p.m., our work would end, and at five p.m., we would all come together for Holy Hour. The four o'clock hour was a kind of free time. You could take a little nap, get some coffee, do extra reading, or exercise. In religious life, but especially in novitiate, there was very little "me time," which made the four o'clock hour a precious commodity.

So, on this day at the beginning of my novitiate, as the clock moved to 3:40 p.m., I said to Fr. Dominic, the novice master, "Hey, Father, do you think it's time for us to start putting things back so we can have the four o'clock hour?" He understood the real motivation behind my question, seeing that I was clinging to this hour of "me time." Fr. Dominic saw in me a bit of selfishness and a desire for comfort that needed to die. So he just looked at me and asked, "What four o'clock hour?" and then pressed us on, working until about 4:50, ten minutes before Holy Hour and leaving me absolutely zero "me time."

Over the course of our novitiate, he pushed all of us to grow, helped us to die to ourselves and not be pulled down by all of the baggage of past experiences. But this was not entirely welcome. At times, I can remember feeling a certain amount of anger, resentment, and frustration. It felt difficult to experience these acts as acts of love.

Then came the morning when we would profess our first vows. For a full year as novices, we had been pushed, stretched, and invited to die to ourselves so that we could enter more deeply into the interior life. On this morning, Fr. Dominic brought all of the novices into the chapel. There, in front of the Blessed Sacrament, he asked us to take off our sandals, and he knelt down with a bowl of water. One by one, he washed our feet, dried them, and then he kissed them.

At that moment, a light turned on inside me. This man, who was about forty years my senior, had pushed himself as he had pushed us. He had been with us in the trenches—in the sweat, in the long hours, in the rain and sleet. He led by example, working alongside us. He did this as an act of love and service because he wanted to give us the gift of maturity. He wanted to give us the gift of freedom and the capacity to give our lives away. He knew that for us to find our lives, we first had to learn how to give them away.

In kneeling before us so humbly, Fr. Dominic was saying, "Thank you for letting me serve you in this way. Please know that it was for love of you and for your good that I pushed you in ways I may not have wanted to push you. I loved you when it was hard, even when I might have wanted to take a break." Immediately, tears of gratitude began to stream down my face.

As we walked out of the chapel, we were prepared to consecrate our lives to God. We were men who had been made new during novitiate; we had been given the capacity to act with maturity and real freedom in taking the vows of poverty, chastity, and obedience in the Franciscan Order.

God's Word

"Truly, truly I say to you, unless a grain of wheat falls into the earth and dies, it remains alone; but if it dies, it bears much fruit. He who loves his life loses it, and he who hates his life in this world will keep it for eternal life. If any one serves me, he must follow me; and where I am, there shall my servant be also; if any one serves me, the Father will honor him" (John 12:24–26).

What It Means for Us

As Jesus walked by the shores of Galilee, he spoke to Simon and Andrew, "Follow me, and I will make you fishers of men" (Matthew 4:19). Certainly, he called his apostles to a particular intimacy with him so that he might love them and care for them. But, as we know, nearly all of the first apostles would be called to martyrdom. When Jesus calls us to a particular vocation—to marriage or to religious life—he calls us to enter a school of love that forces us to face ourselves and to die to ourselves.

The cross of Christ is not a contradiction to the Father's goodness and love of our Father. Rather, his love is often manifest through the crosses he allows in our lives. These experiences are invitations to purification and sanctification. While our good Father does not desire our pain and struggle for its own sake, he does seek the healing and holiness that can come through it.

In our CFR community, if the novices were pampered and protected from daily crosses, they would be unable to do hard things and give their lives away. As a result, they would ultimately experience sadness and disappointment in religious life. They would be unable to live the way they had been called to as a Franciscan. Without learning to die, they would never learn a new way to live.

The truth remains that unless a grain of wheat dies, it remains only a grain of wheat. But if it dies, it bears much fruit (see John 12:24–26). We can only find our lives by giving them away. True joy and perfection require us to go through the Cross and die to ourselves.

There is something powerful and mysterious in Jesus' washing the apostles' feet at the Last Supper. He called them, knowing that with this invitation would come a sharing in the Cross. As he washed their feet, he was saying to them, "Trust me."

May we recognize in our own lives that our heavenly Father gives us crosses and trials for love of us—and that he is always present with us in the midst of them.

Let us pray.

Heavenly Father, anchored in your goodness, help us to trust that the crosses you give us are for our good and our sanctification. Awaken our desires for holiness and magnanimity that we may, with great courage, receive and carry the crosses, purifications, and invitations to give our lives away that come to us each day, especially in the state of life each of us is called to. We ask this in Jesus' name.

Amen.

A Place to Reflect

_____

_____

_____

_____

_____

_____

_____

_____

_____

_____

_____

_____

_____

_____

_____

_____

_____

_____

_____

_____

_____

_____

_____

_____

_____

_____

_____

24

AUTHORITY

As we have seen, each year, Fr. Innocent, our postulant director, takes the postulants on a backpacking trip in the Moab desert. It is a serious endeavor that has a certain degree of risk, so the men are accompanied by two wilderness guides. They have the proper certifications so that, in case of an emergency, they know advanced first aid and can save someone's life if necessary. They are there to ensure that the men stay safe in this rugged environment. They take their job very seriously.

One of the ways they ensure the men's safety is to enforce safety protocols, such as how close one can get to a cliff edge. In addition, the guides help the group navigate the terrain, and they keep an eye on the men's hydration and nutrition.

One day, we were doing a fairly short hike of five miles. As we arrived at our destination in the middle of the afternoon, one of the postulants—who had some serious experience in the wilderness before becoming a friar—passed out.

Quickly, the guides went over and checked on him. As it became clear he wasn't immediately returning to consciousness, they assumed a new role. They were no longer just mentors and brothers; they were now medics and lifesavers. With clear authority, they took ownership of the group and directed us.

As five minutes became ten, and ten minutes became an hour, the guides monitored the unconscious man's vitals to ensure that he was all right and discerned the next step. They decided that he needed to be airlifted to a hospital for treatment. As time passed, some of the men began to engage in some nervous chatter. The noise was distracting the guides from being able to clearly communicate with each other. With authority, one of the guides shouted, "Do not speak when we are helping a patient, do you understand?" The postulants realized their error and immediately became quiet and focused.

Eventually, the helicopter came, and the guides facilitated what needed to be done to get the unconscious man safely onboard. The rescue was successful, and the postulant recovered fully.

There is a time for softness and sweetness, but there is also a time for strength, clarity, and authority, especially when it comes to the safety and salvation of one entrusted to a father's care.

God's Word

"From that time Jesus began to show his disciples that he must go to
Jerusalem and suffer many things from the elders and chief
priests and scribes, and be killed, and on the third day be raised.
And Peter took him and began to rebuke him, saying, 'God forbid,
Lord! This shall never happen to you.' But he turned and said to
Peter, 'Get behind me, Satan! You are a hindrance to me; for you
are not on the side of God, but of men'" (Matthew 16:21–23).

What It Means for Us

There are some moments in the life of Jesus—especially when he spoke with authority—that can make us uncomfortable. As we can understand why the wilderness guides spoke with firmness and authority when one's life was at risk, we can also see why Jesus, who reveals God the Father, might do this. The guides' discipline and directness were motivated by their immediate understanding of the gravity of the situation and the dignity of the life entrusted to their care.

We see Jesus' authority in the cleansing of the Temple. His overturning the tables of the moneychangers and chasing them out can make us uncomfortable. Similarly, some of Jesus' tense interactions with the Pharisees may shake us up a bit. But his response in these situations was correct because it was in accord with what was at stake. Ultimately, it was directed at justice and the protection of those who were being led astray by false teachers and corrupt moneychangers. It was about salvation.

Then, there is the encounter between Jesus and Peter when he told the apostles that he would suffer and die for the salvation of the world. Peter began to contradict Jesus, saying that this would not happen. But Jesus rebukes him, saying, "Get behind me, Satan" (Matthew 16:23). Peter was trying to propose an alternate way of saving humanity, but Jesus knew his mission and the task of salvation that had been given to him by the Father. So, he was clear and authoritative in setting Peter (and the other apostles) straight on the issue.

We can feel emboldened by the strength Jesus showed in these words. We can feel encouraged when others, acting with the grace of Jesus, also boldly proclaim the truth. Proper authority is to be respected, and one who has authority should be firm and protective in exercising it, especially when this authority concerns the protection and salvation of others.

True authority is not an exercise of ego or power. As St. Paul tells us, all authority ultimately comes from God (see Romans 13:1). It is a share in the authority of our heavenly Father, which is manifested in the life, death, and resurrection of his Son, and continued through the Magisterium of the Church. True authority is not soft; it is salvific.

Let us pray.

Heavenly Father, give us the grace to surrender to your authority and to be more receptive to your discipline. Help us to be more attentive to your words and your promptings as you lead us from sin into salvation. We ask this in Jesus' name.

Amen.

A Place to Reflect

25

PERFECT TIMING

When Brad was a junior in college, a Navy recruitment officer came to campus. Growing up post 9/11, patriotism and a desire to serve were deep in Brad's heart. Entering the Navy resonated with his desires, except for one. Brad's only sister, who was two years younger, was pregnant. The father of the child, learning of the pregnancy, had left and made it clear that he wasn't coming back.

Since Brad had been raised in a good home and had grown up to be a good man, he felt a duty to be there to care for his sister and her baby. But he also had a desire to serve his country, and he struggled with this desire. If he joined the Navy, there was no telling where he would be stationed for several years and how much time he would be at sea. He would not be around to be present in his niece's life and to be the influence he wished to be.

In the end, to help him decide what to do, Brad sought the counsel of a wise a priest, who told him, "Brad, remember, when God is asking you for something, it's going to be for your good and for the good of all those involved." This invitation to trust grabbed Brad's heart. So, he decided to join the Navy. As he had expected, he ended up being stationed on ships and bases throughout the world, sometimes for six months at a time.

But he did not forget his niece, Alyssa. Every month, from the time she was a baby, he would write her a letter. In each letter, he would briefly tell her what he was doing in his life, and he would share what he had recently heard about her or her growth. After sharing experiences on his journeys through the oceans of the world, he would write about her first words, her first steps, her First Communion. Each month, without fail, Brad's letters communicated to his niece how much he cared about her, how he loved her, how he missed her, and how he was praying for her. But he did not actually send the letters to his niece; he keeps them in a notebook, intending to give them to her on her eighteenth birthday, which is still a couple years away.

Since Alyssa could be tempted to interpret his absence from her life as indifference, Brad wrote all his letters to assure her that, wherever he was in the world, he was thinking about her. When he presents these to her, as she embarks on adult life, Alyssa will know that she had been in her uncle's thoughts and heart all along—even if she had not been aware of it.

This story can help us understand God the Father's heart. We might not always experience his closeness to us, his loving presence in our lives, especially during difficult times. In those moments, we might ask, "Where are you, God? Why is this happening? Why aren't you healing this situation?" In the Gospel, we read about a man who had been born blind—and who had been suffering his entire life—who then experiences Jesus' healing.

God's Word

"As he passed by, he saw a man blind from his birth ... [and] he spat on the ground and made clay of the spittle and anointed the man's eyes with the clay, saying to him, 'Go, wash in the pool of Siloam' (which means Sent). So he went and washed and came back seeing ... Jesus heard that they had cast him out, and

having found him he said, 'Do you believe in the Son of man?' He answered, 'And who is he, sir, that I may believe in him?' Jesus said to him, 'You have seen him, and it is he who speaks to you.' He said, 'Lord, I believe'; and he worshiped him" (John 9:1, 6–7, 35–38).

What It Means for Us

In his healing, the blind man was not just given physical sight. His miraculous healing opened the door for him to see and receive the Messiah, while many of his peers at that time missed the truth of Jesus. God was pursuing this man, though he did not know it. God had a plan, and in this gift of healing, his plan for the man born blind came to light. If the man had not experienced blindness, would he have been able to recognize Jesus when he encountered him? It was his struggle that put him in the exact spot where Jesus would find him, and when he found him, the man could recognize in the face of Jesus, his savior.

This "happy fault" type of reality plays itself out in our homeless shelter again and again. No one's plan for their life is to end up in a homeless shelter. Surely on the path down that led them to us, they were asking God to stop the decline or help them get on their feet. Nonetheless, countless times, it is when they are with us at their lowest, that men meet Jesus for the first time and come to faith in him. There are numerous stories of men going from the streets to the sacraments in their six months with us at the shelter. Even on the streets, even in their addictions, God was with them and was lovingly maneuvering to save them.

I think this communicates an important and certain truth—God is always at work. He is at work "below the surface" and "behind the scenes," pursuing us and loving us, preparing us to spend our lives with him. Just as Brad was loving and caring for his niece all through her life, God is at work in our lives. Similarly, a plant's roots may grow under the soil for an extended period before any shoots appear above the soil.

The invitation from our Father is to trust him, believing that he is at work and that he responds to all the sufferings and difficulties we experience. We are called to trust that his timing is perfect, and his pursuit of us is ongoing.

As on her eighteenth birthday, Alyssa's eyes will be opened to the ways her uncle was always thinking of her and loving her, we believe that there will be a moment, perhaps not in this life but in the next, when we will see how God was seeing us and loving us along our journey. Then we will understand fully that he never abandoned us but has always loved us and has been lovingly writing the story of our lives.

Let us pray.

Heavenly Father, may we trust that you are at work below the soil, in heights above our imagining, and in whispers too quiet for us to hear. May we trust that you truly are at work loving us and pursuing us, preparing something beautiful for us. Through your grace, may we receive the confidence and ability and patience to give you time, until in your perfect timing and wisdom, your plan is revealed and your love is fully brought to light. We ask this in Jesus' name.

Amen.

A Place to Reflect

26

A FATHER'S DISCIPLINE

To this day, probably the most difficult experience I have had as a friar was my encounter with a man named Gabriel. At the time, I was assigned to the CFR's homeless shelter in the South Bronx. Working with a local organization, this shelter served men who stay with us for up to six months. Gabriel had been coming for more than four months, and he was always quiet and kind. He never caused any problems.

Though I was one of the friars in charge of the shelter, I did not sleep there. One Thursday night, I was on duty, welcoming in the guests for the night, including Gabriel, and I had a nice little chat with him. On Friday morning, when I came back to the shelter for the day, the friar who had been on duty overnight pulled me aside. He told me that he had learned from some of the men that Gabriel had been smuggling in heroin and sneaking into the bathroom in the middle of night to use it. The friar then said that he had actually caught Gabriel in the act.

Of course, we have a strict no tolerance policy for drug use in the shelter. This policy helps protect all the men who are present. We hold our guests accountable, because many of them come to the shelter for help getting sober and remaining clean. If they come in seeming impaired or fail a breathalyzer, we sometimes ask them to take a night or two out.

Since Gabriel had been actually smuggling in drugs and using them, we were going to have to ask him to leave the shelter.

But Gabriel is our brother. He is somebody who God brought us to journey with. It really broke my heart that, due to his drug use in the shelter, he was no longer going to be able to stay with us but would have to go back to the streets.

When I told Gabriel this news, I was moved by his response. He just looked at me and simply said, "I'm sorry. I've been doing this, and I know I shouldn't. And I know that I have to leave."

There was something about his humility, his acceptance, and his ownership that broke my heart even more. But we helped Gabriel pack up his things, and he went off to what is called a "drop-in" shelter for the evening.

Three months went by. I prayed for Gabriel, and I would ask the other men in the shelter how he was doing, but they said that they did not really see him around anymore. Then, while I was on duty one evening helping prepare dinner, the doorbell rang, and Gabriel was standing at the door. I could not have been happier to see him. He had a smile on his face, and he looked great.

Gabriel shared with me that, since he had left us, he had become sober and was able to get into another shelter. He said that he was taking steps to getting housing and a job. He said, "Thank you. I know it was hard, and it has been the best thing for me. So, brother, I'm just really grateful for you guys here and the work you're doing. It's been a huge blessing in my life."

Perhaps one of the most difficult truths for us to accept about the heart of the Father is the relationship between his mercy and his justice. He wants to "spoil" us, his children, to give us what we want—and when we fail, he is merciful to us again and again. But he is also just and upholds his law to protect us.

God's Word

> "[God] desires all men to be saved and to come to the knowledge of the
> truth" (1 Timothy 2:4).

> "It is for discipline that you have to endure. God is treating you as sons
> ... he disciplines us for our good, that we may share his holiness.
> For the moment all discipline seems painful rather than pleasant;
> later it yields the peaceful fruit of righteousness to those who have
> been trained by it" (Hebrews 12:7, 10–11).

What It Means for Us

The Lord does not desire that any of us be lost. There are consequences
to our actions, and these consequences are invitations to repentance.
These consequences are invitations to understand that our choices have
real effects in the world. They are invitations for us to recognize that our
actions affect not only us as individuals but others as well.

Scripture tells us that God desires us all to be saved (see 1 Timothy
2:4). Scripture also tells us that a good father disciplines his children (see
Hebrews 12:6). Our heavenly Father does not want to punish us, but he
does so for our salvation. He wants us to be whole.

When I discovered Gabriel's drug use, I did not want to kick him out
of the shelter. But in this painful situation, I knew that I should trust that
this consequence of his actions was going to be best in the long term for
Gabriel. It was the right remedy for the illness.

In asking Gabriel to leave, I also needed to protect the other men who
were staying with us. I had to be a father to Gabriel and to the other men
as well. God loves us and is a father to each of us as individuals, but he also
loves us and is a father to all of us communally.

As we pray about or discern what to do in certain situations, there can
be a tendency to focus on ourselves or the individual we are concerned

about. But my experience with Gabriel at the shelter, like the experience of fathers in general, can help us learn to see differently. Fathers always have to keep everybody in mind, seeing how an action toward one of their children will affect the rest.

Let us be renewed today in being open to God's discipline. Let us recognize that his discipline is always the right remedy for our moral ailment and at the service of the whole community. He wants us to learn and to repent. He desires that everything we experience may bring us closer to him. Let us trust that he knows what is best for all of us and that he provides what we need so that we can be whole in soul and body, irreproachable at the coming of our Lord Jesus Christ.

Let us pray.

Heavenly Father, it can be hard to experience your discipline, to experience the consequences of our actions. May we be renewed in our trust of you, knowing that you do not desire any of us to be hurt but that you discipline us because of your great love for us. Help us to trust that these painful experiences are at the service of our own repentance, our relationship with you, and our eternal salvation. We ask this in Jesus' name.

Amen.

A Place to Reflect

27

SHATTERED

At school, Joseph heard some of his fifth-grade classmates and some older kids talking about pornography. He became curious about it, and his interest was piqued as he heard them describing what they saw, in pictures and videos on the Internet.

At home, Joseph's parents did everything they could to keep their kids safe from pornography. All televisions, computers, and screens were in common areas of the house—with the exception of a couple of Kindles. What Joseph's father didn't know was that a Kindle, which is primarily designed to display the text of books, could also show images. As a ten-year-old, Joseph searched for pornographic images one night. Though he felt ashamed, he also was excited by it. Over the next six months, he viewed pornography on a regular basis.

Joseph's excitement quickly turned to a feeling of constant shame and guilt. He knew better. His parents had taught him that viewing pornography was harmful and something that members of his family did not do.

One night, wanting to come clean but terrified to tell his father what he had been doing, Joseph finally confessed all that he had been doing to his father through tears. Joseph's dad just gently took him by the arm, pulled him to his chest in a hug, and said, "Joseph, I love you. I'm so proud of you for coming to me and being honest. It breaks my heart that you saw these things and experienced this shame, but I want you to know that I love you and am proud of you for being honest with me. It takes a lot of courage to tell the truth."

Joseph went to bed that night still experiencing the shame of what he had done but also reflecting on the depths of his father's love and care for him. He was moved by how lovingly and mercifully his father had received him as he shared his struggle.

The next morning, Joseph peeked in his dad's study to say goodbye as he left for school. Out of the corner of his eye, he saw both Kindles in the trash can, shattered and broken in pieces. While his father had been deeply merciful toward his son, the sinner, he had been extremely zealous and quick in destroying the object that was hurting his son.

God's Word

> *"Whoever receives one such child in my name receives me; but whoever causes one of these little ones who believe in me to sin, it would be better for him to have a great millstone fastened round his neck and to be drowned in the depth of the sea. Woe to the world for temptations to sin! ... And if your hand or your foot causes you to sin, cut it off and throw it from you; it is better for you to enter life maimed or lame than with two hands or two feet to be thrown into the eternal fire" (Matthew 18:5–8).*

What It Means for Us

The Gospels repeatedly give us insight into Jesus' heart as he welcomes the sinner and eats and drinks with tax collectors. God is stunningly merciful and compassionate toward sinners. When we return to him again and again for his forgiveness, he always receives us with tenderness. He shows us we can always return to him.

At the same time, Jesus flipped over the tables of the moneychangers to cleanse the Temple. While Jesus continues to love the sinner and to be merciful and compassionate toward us, he is aggressive and zealous toward that which causes us to sin. He is not indifferent to sin. He is not indifferent to the suffering of his children or their innocence. He cares about the hearts of his children, and he will fight to protect us.

Joseph's father received him and was merciful toward him. At the same time, as a good father, he was quick to root out and destroy what was hurting his son. In his own words, Jesus communicates this same mercy and justice to us as he says, "And if your right hand causes you to sin, cut it off and throw it away; it is better that you lose one of your members than that your whole body go into hell" (Matthew 5:30). He also says that whoever causes others to sin would be better off having a millstone thrown around their necks and be tossed into the ocean (see Matthew 18:6). These words can seem intimidating and aggressive, but when we understand that Jesus has the heart of a father, they make sense. He desires to protect us and to care for us. He is not indifferent toward our sin.

Let us prayerfully consider if there is anything in our lives that we need to cut out. This could be the way we use technology or social media, or how we look at others' lives and become jealous. Is there anything that needs to be removed to protect our own hearts or to protect the hearts of our children or those entrusted to our care? We need to trust the Lord wants to help us root these things out of our lives because he loves us.

Let us pray.

Heavenly Father, we are moved by your ability to be compassionate to us in our sinfulness and our weakness, while being zealous in your desire to protect us and remove any instruments, structures, or behaviors that cause us to sin. You are firm in breaking down those things that lead us to lose our innocence and our sense of identity as your beloved children, which cause us to experience shame and sadness. Lord, we again give you permission to root out whatever it is in our lives that is causing us to sin and cleanse the temple of our hearts. Help us to trust in your love and care for us. We ask this in Jesus' name.

Amen.

A Place to Reflect

28

A HEART FOR THE POOR

One of the rules of the Franciscan Friars of the Renewal is to live in an area noted for the poverty. If a neighborhood's economic status improves too much—that is, becomes "gentrified," to use a popular term—we will move to a poorer area. The reason is that we always want to be in a place where the poor can come to our door. So it is common in our friaries for the doorbell to ring throughout the day.

Early one Tuesday evening, as we were making our daily holy hour of Eucharistic Adoration, the doorbell rang. It was my job during Adoration to answer the door on the first ring. When I got there, I saw one of our neighbors who came regularly to the friary. Her name was Ashley. We had gotten to know her story, and we knew that she was alone in the area, living in government housing. It had been really heart-wrenching to watch Ashley decline over the previous few months. Part of the tragedy of her life was her addiction to drugs, and it was taking a toll on her body. By this point, her hands were constantly shaking.

Ashley was at the door asking for something to eat. We had a pot of soup on the stove that was being prepared for the friars' dinner, so I put some soup in a bowl and made her a grilled cheese sandwich that she could take to go. I brought the food out to her and then went to get her a cup of coffee.

When I brought her the coffee, I saw that she was struggling to eat the soup because of her shaking hands, which broke my heart. So I asked if I could help her in some way. She said, "Well, you could feed it to me." So, I stepped out of the door and took the bowl and spoon from her. I took a spoonful of the soup, held it in front of her mouth so she could blow on it to cool down, and then gave it to her. Slowly but surely, I fed soup to this sixty-five-year-old woman like a father would feed one of his young children.

There was not much talking as she ate. What I noticed most was the movement of my heart. To be honest, not once, even for the slightest moment, did any of Ashley's struggles with addiction come to my mind as I fed her, bite after bite. I just experienced how this sweet woman, in her need, delighted my heart by allowing me to help care for her in her poverty.

God's Word

> "*Thus says the* LORD: *Heaven is my throne and the earth is my*
>   *footstool ...*
>   *But this is the man to whom I will look, he that is humble and*
>   *contrite in spirit,*
>   *and trembles at my word*" (Isaiah 66:1–2).

What It Means for Us

The Gospels provide us with several accounts in which Jesus allows someone to come close, and those around him point out that he is allowing a sinful person to approach him. In Luke 5, we hear about how Jesus calls Levi, a tax collector, who responds by inviting the Lord to a feast in his home at which other public sinners are present. The Pharisees indignantly ask, "Why do you eat and drink with tax collectors and sinners?" And

Jesus' response is, "Those who are well have no need of a physician, but those who are sick; I have not come to call the righteous, but sinners to repentance" (see Luke 5:27–32). Again, one of the Pharisees invites Jesus to a meal, and a woman enters the room and kisses his feet. Although the Pharisee thinks that Jesus will reject her because of her sinfulness, Jesus tells him, "I tell you, her sins, which are many, are forgiven, for she loved much" (see Luke 7:36–50).

It is not that Jesus is indifferent toward sin; rather, he always sees the sinner as his son or daughter. The Pharisee thought that Jesus would not allow the sinful woman to come near and anoint his feet because she was a sinner. But when Jesus received this gesture of love from this poor, struggling woman, he did not see her as a sinner and reject her. He saw only his daughter, and he forgave her because of her great love. Similarly, when Jesus converses with the Samaritan woman at the well, he knows she is a sinner. But he speaks to her because he loves her; she is his beloved daughter (see John 4:5–30).

As Jesus reveals the Father, our invitation today is to recognize that he knows our struggles and loves us in our poverty. These accounts in the Gospel are a reminder that our Father knows our difficulties and addictions, but he does not identify us by them. He is deeply moved by our poverty and seeks to make us rich in his grace and love.

In the book of the prophet Isaiah, the Lord says, "This is the man to whom I will look, he that is humble and contrite in spirit, and trembles at my word" (Isaiah 66:2). God calls us to come to him, and he will never reject a broken, contrite heart. If my own heart was moved by the privilege of caring for Ashley in her need, how much more is the infinite love and mercy of our heavenly Father waiting for us in our need.

In the Gospels, Jesus gives us a model of prayer, telling us not to be like the Pharisee who congratulates himself for obeying the law but rather to be like the sinner who cannot even bring himself to raise his eyes to heaven, saying, "Be merciful to me a sinner" (Luke 18:13).

When we experience our own brokenness of spirit, may we turn to God. May our struggles not be a cause for us to keep Jesus away. May we bring our brokenness to him, because he truly wants to care for us in our humility and our dependence on him. He does not see us as sinners and addicts and reject us but as his beloved sons and daughters.

Let us pray.

Heavenly Father, the temptation of our brokenness and poverty is to hide from you and to try to heal it on our own. The temptation is to wait to come to you after we have got things together. May we experience again the truth that you want us to come to in all of our mess, in all of our struggles. May our experience of our brokenness lead us to turn to you, knowing that your Son came not for the healthy but the sick, to save us poor sinners. We ask this in Jesus' name.

Amen.

A Place to Reflect

_____

_____

_____

_____

_____

_____

_____

_____

_____

_____

_____

_____

_____

29

END WELL

When the friars first met Julissa in Honduras, she was about six years old. They were working in her neighborhood, and they got to know her as we helped her mother. Through a series of unfortunate events, Julissa's mother had become addicted to alcohol and turned to prostitution to help pay for her addiction and provide income for her family.

Over the years, as Julissa's mother came in and out of the scene, Julissa was primarily taken care of by her aunts or other members of the local Catholic parish. She got involved with the youth group, but as she grew up, slowly but surely, the effects of her mother's life began to draw her to the streets as well. In her early teens, she started to get into trouble with drugs and alcohol, promiscuity, and then prostitution.

She would go to work on the streets, then she would return after a few months. The friars, as well as some other missionaries with whom they worked, would help her for a while, but soon she would return to the streets. This became the pattern Julissa would follow over the next ten years.

The brothers, the local parish, and the missionaries had done everything they could to help Julissa stay clean, get an education, and have a better, healthier life. But nothing they did seemed to work. Finally,

Julissa disappeared for several years, as addiction and brokenness took over all aspects of her life.

In time, the brothers received the sad news that Julissa had become sick. Although she was still in her early twenties, her health was declining quickly. Eventually, it became clear that she only had a few days left to live as her addiction and poor living conditions left her immune system severely compromised.

The friars and the neighbors visited and prayed with Julissa and gave her consolation in the final days of her earthly life. When she was offered the opportunity to receive the sacraments of the Anointing of the Sick, Reconciliation, and Holy Communion, she said yes. So, a few days before her final breath, Julissa received the fullness of the mercy of God poured out through the sacraments of the Church. She received God's healing and forgiveness and was restored to grace, as she was given the gift of what Catholics call a "happy death."

Through the persistent generosity and love of the friars and many other Catholics in the neighborhood, Julissa knew that she was being invited to return to her loving Father through the sacraments. Because of their care, when she was offered a chance to return to the Church, Julissa knew she was being called by a God who is merciful and compassionate. The Father's voice had become a familiar voice and his face a welcoming gaze. The Church's care paved the way for her to receive his mercy with confidence.

God's Word

> "And he said to him, 'Truly, I say to you, today you will be with me in Paradise'" (Luke 23:43).

What It Means for Us

Catholics often refer to St. Dismas as the "Good Thief." He was one of the two men crucified along with our Lord, who in the last moments of his life recognized that Jesus was the Messiah. With perhaps his last words, Dismas called out to Jesus, asking for his mercy and forgiveness. In return, he heard the most beautiful words: "Today you will be with me in Paradise" (Luke 23:43).

God never ceases to pursue us. This is good news for our lives, and it is good news for the lives of those we love. The Father was willing to pursue us even though it meant his Son would be nailed to and die on the Cross so that he could be "next to us" and save us from our sins. We know that God never ceases to pursue us and will go to any lengths to save us.

Dismas' loved ones must have been concerned about him. After all, he lived a wayward life that ultimately led him to be condemned to execution. Surely, they were anxious and discouraged about the possibility of him ever meeting God. How many of our loved ones, perhaps some of our siblings or children, do we watch with concern as we see them not following the Lord? May the story of Julissa and the story of St. Dismas give us confidence that God the Father never ceases to pursue us. May it give us the courage to persevere in continuing to love those who are struggling, to pray for them, and to offer sacrifices for them. While our care for them and our prayers may not change the way they live, they may change the way they die.

Let us pray.

Heavenly Father, may your pursuit of the Good Thief give us confidence that you never cease to pursue us. May it also fill us with supernatural hope for all those we love and care about, especially those farthest from you and most in need of your mercy. May our prayers and sacrifices on their behalf win for them and for all of us the grace of a happy death. We ask this in Jesus' name.

Amen.

A Place to Reflect

_____
_____
_____
_____
_____
_____
_____
_____
_____
_____
_____
_____
_____
_____
_____
_____
_____
_____
_____
_____
_____
_____
_____
_____
_____

30

HE LAID DOWN HIS LIFE

Thomas "Tom" Vander Woude, whom his grandkids called Papa, loved all his sons with a deep and sacrificial love. But his youngest son, Joseph, referred to affectionately as Josie, had a special place in his heart and in the hearts of the entire family. Part of what gave Josie this special place was the fact that he was born with Down syndrome.

Mr. Vander Woude was a "man's man." He was an athlete and a coach; he ran every day and handed on this discipline to his sons, who carried on the Vander Woude legacy in sports. But with Josie, Tom's athleticism and discipline were manifested not in competing for a championship but in more profound ways.

Having Down syndrome meant that some of Josie's development was different from other children. One activity Josie struggled with but needed to learn because of how it helped brain development, was crawling. So, to be able to spend as much time as possible with Josie teaching him how to crawl, Tom had special socks and pads made allowing him to spend hours crawling beside his son.

One of the gifts of Josie's situation was that he was usually at home. So, over the years, when Tom was working on the family farm, Josie would often go outside and spend time with his dad. The day that tragedy would strike began like any other day. Tom had woken up early and gone to daily Mass which, along with the daily Rosary, were the foundation of his life. Then he went to work on the farm, inviting Josie to join him. While he was working, Tom suddenly heard an alarming sound of cracking and breaking. What had broken was the lid to the septic cistern, and Josie had fallen in. Without hesitation, Tom dove into the cistern, took hold of Josie, and held him up so he could breathe.

Mrs. Vander Woude, alerted to what had happened, immediately called 911 and cried out to God. She ran to them and could see the heartbreaking sight of Josie barely hanging on in the cistern. From above, she did her best to help keep Josie up, but in the struggle to save Josie, through exhaustion and due to the toxic gases, Tom eventually lost consciousness and fell below the sewage level. Josie would survive and make a full recovery, but Tom wouldn't survive.

At his wake, the line to pay respects to Tom went on for hours. The perpetual adoration chapel where he had made a weekly Holy Hour from two to three a.m. (choosing that time because it was one of the toughest shifts) was renamed for him. His sons, one of whom is a Catholic priest, to this day keep the tradition of making a weekly Holy Hour at two o'clock in the morning in honor of their father.

Fr. Vander Woude once shared that perhaps some might look at a healthy father losing his life to save a son with Down syndrome as a waste. But for Mr. Vander Woude, Josie was simply his son, and he would have freely laid down his life to save any of his children.

It was at the close of a FOCUS recruitment weekend that I first heard this story from one of Tom's granddaughters. In many ways, hearing this example of the love of this good father for his son was the spark that led to this book of meditations, as it led me to reflect on the way a father's love can lead us to the heart of God the Father.

The Father loves his sons and daughters so deeply, and he desires our salvation so viscerally, that he sent his Son, Jesus, to die for us.

God's Word

"By this we know love, that he laid down his life for us" (1 John 3:16).

"Have this mind among yourselves, which was in Christ Jesus, who, though he was in the form of God, did not count equality with God a thing to be grasped, but emptied himself, taking the form of a servant, being born in the likeness of men. And being found in human form he humbled himself and became obedient unto death, even death on a cross. Therefore God has highly exalted him and bestowed on him the name which is above every name, that at the name of Jesus every knee should bow, in heaven and on earth and under the earth, and every tongue confess that Jesus Christ is Lord, to the glory of God the Father" (Philippians 2:5–11).

What It Means for Us

There is no indifference in the heart of God for his children. In the parable of the Prodigal Son, we read that the father, seeing his son at a distance, ran to him, embraced him, kissed him, and rejoiced that his son who was lost had been found. This pursuit of the father for his children is not just a parable; it is a historical reality. It is the reality of the incarnation, life, death, and resurrection of Jesus to save us.

Jesus freely emptied himself, leaving the right hand of the Father. Born in Bethlehem and growing up in Nazareth, he literally crawled among us. He spent his whole life pursuing each of us. Ultimately, he took upon himself all of the sewage and mess—that is, all of the sin—of humanity.

As Mr. Vander Woude freely laid down his life for his son, so it is true in an even more exemplary way that Jesus Christ died for you and for me.

He took our sin upon himself and freely laid down his life so that you and I, poor and weak and insignificant as we are, could be saved. He died for us so we could have the opportunity of spending eternity in heaven with him.

Why? Because nothing is more significant to our loving Father than his children. He knows you, loves you, and desires you to be with him forever. In the end, this is the most important truth you could ever wrestle with and the most important gift you could ever receive: your Father's love.

Let us pray.

Heavenly Father, may your passion for me free me from any temptation to doubt my value in the world. May the depths you were willing to go in pursuit of me move my heart to gratitude, but also to contrition and repentance for times I have doubted or rejected your love for me. Help me to receive the gift of your pursuit of me. I ask this in Jesus' name.

Amen.

A Place to Reflect

CONCLUSION
"Abba, Father"

We have concluded our journey together. These thirty meditations have led the way along a journey dedicated to contemplating the truth that we call God "Abba, Father." We have wrestled with that truth and the effects of it. Knowing who he is changes everything.

May God's fatherhood continue to comfort us, strengthen us, and be our place of refuge and confidence. In all things, may we never forget his delight in us and his investment in our lives. May we never forget his care for us and his patience and persistence in pursuing and forgiving us. May we never forget his love for us.

May confidence in the goodness of God our Father be our source of trust and confidence when his ways do not match up with our ways and his timeline does not match up with ours. As the difficulties of life challenge our faith and our limits, may we always cry out to our heavenly Father.

God the Father sent his only begotten Son, Jesus, to establish the Church so that we could have the fullness of this truth. In this, we can see that we have a heavenly Father who is the best of fathers and who loves us. The Church's teachings and guidance give us the path to enter into and to remain in a relationship with him, receiving grace as we journey through this valley of tears to reach our goal where all will be brought to light and all tears will be wiped away—our heavenly homeland, which is an eternity in the very heart of our Father.

Let us pray.

Heavenly Father, you have revealed to us that we are beloved children. May we remember this truth. May we not go about this life for even one moment alone or in doubt, but may we always remain rooted in the truth that you are our Father, and you are the best of fathers.

Amen.

ACKNOWLEDGMENTS

Any work of mine is the collective fruit of many generous hands and hearts. I can't do this on my own, nor would I want to.

Firstly, I would like to thank Thomas Griffin for his wise and faithful help in getting this project off the ground. Several of the stories included in this book came from Thomas' personal experience and research. Thanks, brother, for your friendship and support—and for always "letting" me win on the court.

Secondly, I would like to thank all of those who shared their stories with me for this work. Thank you all for trusting me and inviting me into intimate and vulnerable parts of your hearts and history. I pray that I was a good steward of what you entrusted to me. Your stories have been profoundly moving insights into God the Father for me and I am confident they will offer the same to the readers.

Finally, a huge thank you to the entire team at Ascension. Working with you continues to be a dream collaboration on every level. Thank you for your ongoing investment in me and for turning my little ideas into occasions of grace for many people. May God reward you.